Spoon River Anthology

BY EDGAR LEE MASTERS

CONTENTS

Spoon River Anthology

BY EDGAR LEE MASTERS

PRESTWICK HOUSE
LITERARY TOUCHSTONE CLASSICS™
P.O. BOX 658 • CLAYTON, DELAWARE 19938

Senior Editor: Paul Moliken

Editors: Lisa M. Miller and Mary Grimes

Cover Design: Larry Knox

Production: Jerry Clark

Prestwick House
Literary Touchstone Classics

P.O. Box 658 • Clayton, Delaware 19938

Tel: 1.800.932.4593

Fax: 1.888.718.9333

Web: www.prestwickhouse.com

Prestwick House Teaching Units™, Activity Packs™, and Response Journals™ are the perfect complement for these editions. To purchase teaching resources for this book, visit www.prestwickhouse.com/material

This Prestwick House edition is an unabridged republication with slight emendations of *Spoon River Anthology,* published in 1919 by The MacMillan Co., New York.

©2007 All new material is copyrighted by Prestwick House, Inc. All rights reserved. No portion may be reproduced without permission in writing from the publisher. Printed in the United States of America.

ISBN 978-1-58049-339-0

NOTES

What is a literary classic and why are these classic works important to the world?

A literary classic is a work of the highest excellence that has something important to say about life and/or the human condition and says it with great artistry. A classic, through its enduring presence, has withstood the test of time and is not bound by time, place, or customs. It speaks to us today as forcefully as it spoke to people one hundred or more years ago, and as forcefully as it will speak to people of future generations. For this reason, a classic is said to have universality.

Edgar Lee Masters was born in Garnett, Kansas, on August 23, 1868. During the first ten years of his life, both a brother and a best friend died, which influenced the young Masters and stimulated his interest in how death affects the living, who are left behind.

In 1880, he and the rest of the family moved to Lewistown, Illinois, near the actual Spoon River.

He married Helen M. Jenkins in 1898, and Masters began to practice law, which he did for nearly thirty years. Intermittently, though, Masters wrote poems, a play, a few novels, and essays. None however achieved nearly the fame of his most popular work, *Spoon River Anthology*, the collection of epitaphs in free verse for which he is most famous. This collection of the secret lives of seemingly ordinary citizens instantly placed Masters in the company of Whitman and other great American poets, at least in the minds of the reading public and some critics. His rightful place among the literary greats, however, is debated, even today.

Later in his life, Masters wrote biographies of Mark Twain, Walt Whitman, and Abe Lincoln. After a bitter divorce and a long fight against pneumonia, Masters married again and moved to New York, where he retired from the law.

Masters died in 1950. He is remembered as a transitional poet, one whose work laid the groundwork for many of the poets of the mid-twentieth century.

Reading Pointers for Sharper Insights

To fully appreciate the complexities found in Edgar Lee Masters' *Spoon River Anthology*, be aware of the following concepts as you read:

1. **Setting:** Imagine a graveyard in Spoon River, Illinois. It is a fictitious, small town, where everyone knows everyone. Many of the characters are actual portrayals of people Masters knew from his own hometown, Lewistown, Illinois, and from his grandparents' town, Petersburg, Illinois. For this anthology, Masters created individual epitaphs for the townspeople.

    Spoon River was a community that longed for perfection. The town officials and many of the townspeople wanted their town to be free of sin and full of faith and goodness. As a result, this conservative town became extremely judgmental, harsh, and conforming, which caused hostility and animosity in some of them.

2. **Epitaphs:**
    *   Masters chose to write the epitaphs using a free verse poetic form; this technique adds to the unique style of Spoon River Anthology.
    *   The inhabitants have written their own epitaph after their death.
    *   The epitaphs are written with honesty, confidence, and are free of shame. During life, everyday facades typically hinder people from telling the whole truth; now that they are dead, they have nothing to fear.
    *   The afterlife is not a typical topic in the epitaphs because the dead seem most concerned with other issues (their gravesite, the way they died, their actions during life, asking for forgiveness, the community, etc.).
    *   Many epitaphs are used to teach a lesson. Those characters who realize the mistakes they made during life, will try to convey that as a warning, but other epitaphs use the way the deceased were treated by the community as examples of how not to live life.
    *   The town of Spoon River was small, so most of the characters knew each other and mention people in their epitaphs.

3. **Themes/Motifs:** Although each epitaph is very different, some are linked through common motifs or themes.
   - **Regret:** The notion of *regret* is alluded to in many epitaphs; however, each individual deals with regret differently. Some may express their regrets as a lesson, hoping to pass experiences on in such a way that the living will not make the same mistakes. Others simply tell their story, expressing their regrets honestly and without shame.
   - **Peace through death:** Many people from Spoon River found peace in death. In some cases, individuals had become lonely or sorrowful, and, therefore, found that death relieved them of those emotions. Others found peace because of the way they lived their lives, so they were able to die with a clear conscience.
   - **Guilt:** Some epitaphs express guilt. Perhaps he or she left behind a significant other, family members, or close friends. The guilt leaves the dead restless and anxious, haunted with the pain of leaving life. Others may experience guilt because of the actions they made through life; they may have lived a life of crime, or committed a grave sin.
   - **Life:** For most of the epitaphs, *life* is the topic. Many epitaphs simply detail the person's daily life before death. In some cases, people may have been ignored during life, and now, through death, they finally have the opportunity to express the way their life was led.
   - **Equality:** Although, *equality* is not alluded to through the words in each epitaph, the overall theme of Masters' work seems to be focused on the graveyard as a whole. Regardless of how the individual chose to live his or her life, each has experienced death, and is now buried beneath the soil in the same yard.

4. **Metaphors/Similes:** There are metaphors and similes included in nearly all the epitaphs in *Spoon River Anthology*. Note that the metaphors take the form of something near and dear to the deceased person. As an example, an avid gardener will metaphorically define life using terms or situations related to gardening. This technique allows the reader to experience each epitaph separately and note how different each individual was.

Spoon River Anthology

The Hill †

WHERE ARE ELMER, Herman, Bert, Tom and Charley,
The weak of will, the strong of arm, the clown, the boozer, the fighter?
All, all are sleeping on the hill.

One passed in a fever,
One was burned in a mine,
One was killed in a brawl,
One died in a jail,
One fell from a bridge toiling for children and wife—
All, all are sleeping, sleeping, sleeping on the hill.

Where are Ella, Kate, Mag, Lizzie and Edith,
The tender heart, the simple soul, the loud, the proud, the happy one?—
All, all are sleeping on the hill.

One died in shameful child-birth,
One of a thwarted love,
One at the hands of a brute in a brothel,
One of a broken pride, in the search for heart's desire,
One after life in far-away London and Paris
Was brought to her little space by Ella and Kate and Mag—
All, all are sleeping, sleeping, sleeping on the hill.

†Terms marked in the text with (†) can be looked up in the Glossary for additional information.

Where are Uncle Isaac and Aunt Emily,
And old Towny Kincaid and Sevigne Houghton,
And Major Walker who had talked
With venerable men of the revolution?—
All, all are sleeping on the hill.

They brought them dead sons from the war,
And daughters whom life had crushed,
And their children fatherless, crying—
All, all are sleeping, sleeping, sleeping on the hill.

Where is Old Fiddler Jones
Who played with life all his ninety years,
Braving the sleet with bared breast,
Drinking, rioting, thinking neither of wife nor kin,
Nor gold, nor love, nor heaven?
Lo! he babbles of the fish-frys of long ago,
Of the horse-races of long ago at Clary's Grove,
Of what Abe Lincoln said
One time at Springfield.

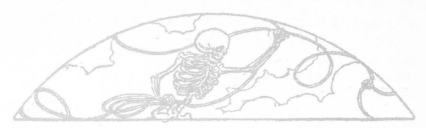

Hod Putt

HERE I LIE close to the grave
Of Old Bill Piersol,
Who grew rich trading with the Indians, and who
Afterwards took the bankrupt law
And emerged from it richer than ever
Myself grown tired of toil and poverty
And beholding how Old Bill and others grew in wealth,
Robbed a traveler one night near Proctor's Grove,
Killing him unwittingly while doing so,
For the which I was tried and hanged.
That was my way of going into bankruptcy.
Now we who took the bankrupt law in our respective ways
Sleep peacefully side by side.†

Ollie McGee

HAVE YOU SEEN walking through the village
A man with downcast eyes and haggard face?
That is my husband who, by secret cruelty
Never to be told, robbed me of my youth and my beauty;
Till at last, wrinkled and with yellow teeth,
And with broken pride and shameful humility,
I sank into the grave.
But what think you gnaws at my husband's heart?
The face of what I was, the face of what he made me!
These are driving him to the place where I lie.
In death, therefore, I am avenged.

Fletcher McGee

SHE TOOK MY strength by minutes,
She took my life by hours,
She drained me like a fevered moon
That saps the spinning world.
The days went by like shadows,
The minutes wheeled like stars.
She took the pity from my heart,
And made it into smiles.
She was a hunk of sculptor's clay,
My secret thoughts were fingers:
They flew behind her pensive brow
And lined it deep with pain.
They set the lips, and sagged the cheeks,
And drooped the eyes with sorrow.
My soul had entered in the clay,
Fighting like seven devils.
It was not mine, it was not hers;
She held it, but its struggles
Modeled a face she hated,
And a face I feared to see.
I beat the windows, shook the bolts.
I hid me in a corner—
And then she died and haunted me,
And hunted me for life.†

Robert Fulton† Tanner

IF A MAN could bite the giant hand
That catches and destroys him,
As I was bitten by a rat
While demonstrating my patent trap,
In my hardware store that day.
But a man can never avenge himself
On the monstrous ogre Life.
You enter the room—that's being born;
And then you must live—work out your soul,
Aha! the bait that you crave is in view:
A woman with money you want to marry,
Prestige, place, or power in the world.
But there's work to do and things to conquer—
Oh, yes! the wires that screen the bait.
At last you get in—but you hear a step:
The ogre, Life, comes into the room,
(He was waiting and heard the clang of the spring)
To watch you nibble the wondrous cheese,
And stare with his burning eyes at you,
And scowl and laugh, and mock and curse you,
Running up and down in the trap,
Until your misery bores him.†

Cassius Hueffer

THEY HAVE CHISELED on my stone the words:
"His life was gentle, and the elements so mixed in him
That nature might stand up and say to all the world,
This was a man."
Those who knew me smile
As they read this empty rhetoric.

My epitaph should have been:
"Life was not gentle to him,
And the elements so mixed in him
That he made warfare on life,
In the which he was slain."
While I lived I could not cope with slanderous tongues,
Now that I am dead I must submit to an epitaph
Graven by a fool!

Serepta Mason

MY LIFE'S BLOSSOM might have bloomed on all sides
Save for a bitter wind which stunted my petals
On the side of me which you in the village could see.
From the dust I lift a voice of protest:
My flowering side you never saw!
Ye living ones, ye are fools indeed
Who do not know the ways of the wind
And the unseen forces
That govern the processes of life.

Amanda Barker

HENRY GOT ME with child,
Knowing that I could not bring forth life
Without losing my own.
In my youth therefore I entered the portals of dust.
Traveler, it is believed in the village where I lived
That Henry loved me with a husband's love,
But I proclaim from the dust
That he slew me to gratify his hatred.

Constance Hately

YOU PRAISE MY self-sacrifice, Spoon River,
In rearing Irene and Mary,
Orphan's of my older sister!
And you censure Irene and Mary
For their contempt for me!
But praise not my self-sacrifice,
And censure not their contempt;
I reared them, I cared for them, true enough!—
But I poisoned my benefactions
With constant reminders of their dependence.

Town Drunkard

Chase Henry — Barker

IN LIFE I was the town drunkard;
When I died the priest denied me burial
In holy ground.
The which redounded to my good fortune.
For the Protestants bought this lot,
And buried my body here,
Close to the grave of the banker Nicholas,
And of his wife Priscilla.
Take note, ye prudent and pious souls,
Of the cross-currents in life
Which bring honor to the dead, who lived in shame.[†]

Harry Carey Goodhue

YOU NEVER MARVELED, dullards of Spoon River,
When Chase Henry voted against the saloons
To revenge himself for being shut off.
But none of you was keen enough
To follow my steps, or trace me home
As Chase's spiritual brother.
Do you remember when I fought
The bank and the courthouse ring,
For pocketing the interest of public funds?
And when I fought our leading citizens
For making the poor the pack-horses of the taxes?
And when I fought the water works
For stealing streets and raising rates?
And when I fought the business men
Who fought me in these fights?
Then do you remember:
That staggering up from the wreck of defeat,
And the wreck of a ruined career,
I slipped from my cloak my last ideal,
Hidden from all eyes until then,
Like the cherished jawbone of an ass,
And smote the bank and the water works,
And the business men with prohibition,
And made Spoon River pay the cost
Of the fights that I had lost.

Discontent, Anger, Revenge

Judge Somers

HOW DOES IT happen, tell me,
That I who was most erudite of lawyers,
Who knew Blackstone[†] and Coke[†]
Almost by heart, who made the greatest speech
The court-house ever heard, and wrote
A brief that won the praise of Justice Breese[†]
How does it happen, tell me,
That I lie here unmarked, forgotten,
While Chase Henry, the town drunkard,
Has a marble block, topped by an urn
Wherein Nature, in a mood ironical,
Has sown a flowering weed?

Restless

Kinsey Keene

YOUR ATTENTION, THOMAS RHODES, president of the bank;
Coolbaugh Whedon, editor of the Argus;
Rev. Peet, pastor of the leading church;
A.D. Blood, several times Mayor of Spoon River;
And finally all of you, members of the Social Purity Club[†]—
Your attention to Cambronne's[†] dying words,
Standing with the heroic remnant
Of Napoleon's[†] guard on Mount Saint Jean
At the battle field of Waterloo,
When Maitland,[†] the Englishman, called to them:
"Surrender, brave Frenchmen!"—
There at close of day with the battle hopelessly lost,
And hordes of men no longer the army
Of the great Napoleon
Streamed from the field like ragged strips
Of thunder clouds in the storm.
Well, what Cambronne said to Maitland
Ere the English fire made smooth the brow of the hill
Against the sinking light of day
Say I to you, and all of you,
And to you, O world.
And I charge you to carve it
Upon my stone.

Benjamin Pantier

TOGETHER IN THIS grave lie Benjamin Pantier, attorney at law,
And Nig, his dog, constant companion, solace and friend.
Down the gray road, friends, children, men and women,
Passing one by one out of life, left me till I was alone
With Nig for partner, bed-fellow, comrade in drink.
In the morning of life I knew aspiration and saw glory.
Then she, who survives me, snared my soul
With a snare which bled me to death,
Till I, once strong of will, lay broken, indifferent,
Living with Nig in a room back of a dingy office.
Under my jaw-bone is snuggled the bony nose of Nig—
Our story is lost in silence. Go by, mad world!

he missed his wife after she kicked him out.
Regret, Remorse

Mrs. Benjamin Pantier

I KNOW THAT he told that I snared his soul
With a snare which bled him to death.
And all the men loved him,
And most of the women pitied him.
But suppose you are really a lady, and have delicate tastes,
And loathe the smell of whiskey and onions,
And the rhythm of Wordsworth's "Ode"[†] runs in your ears,
While he goes about from morning till night
Repeating bits of that common thing;
"Oh, why should the spirit of mortal be proud?"
And then, suppose:
You are a woman well endowed,
And the only man with whom the law and morality
Permit you to have the marital relation
Is the very man that fills you with disgust
Every time you think of it—while you think of it
Every time you see him?
That's why I drove him away from home
To live with his dog in a dingy room
Back of his office.

Anger, Content

Reuben Pantier

WELL, EMILY SPARKS, your prayers were not wasted,
Your love was not all in vain.
I owe whatever I was in life
To your hope that would not give me up,
To your love that saw me still as good.
Dear Emily Sparks, let me tell you the story.
I pass the effect of my father and mother;
The milliner's daughter made me trouble
And out I went in the world,
Where I passed through every peril known
Of wine and women and joy of life.
One night, in a room in the Rue de Rivoli,†
I was drinking wine with a black-eyed cocotte,
And the tears swam into my eyes.
She thought they were amorous tears and smiled
For thought of her conquest over me.
But my soul was three thousand miles away,
In the days when you taught me in Spoon River.
And just because you no more could love me,
Nor pray for me, nor write me letters,
The eternal silence of you spoke instead.
And the Black-eyed cocotte took the tears for hers,
As well as the deceiving kisses I gave her.
Somehow, from that hour, I had a new vision—
Dear Emily Sparks!

Love Lost, Adultery
Unrequited

Emily Sparks — *Reuben Painter*

WHERE IS MY boy, my boy—
In what far part of the world?
The boy I loved best of all in the school?—
I, the teacher, the old maid, the virgin heart,
Who made them all my children.
Did I know my boy aright,
Thinking of him as a spirit aflame,
Active, ever aspiring?
Oh, boy, boy, for whom I prayed and prayed
In many a watchful hour at night,
Do you remember the letter I wrote you
Of the beautiful love of Christ?
And whether you ever took it or not,
My, boy, wherever you are,
Work for your soul's sake,
That all the clay of you, all of the dross of you,
May yield to the fire of you,
Till the fire is nothing but light!…
Nothing but light![†]

Love Unrequited

Trainor, the Druggist — *Pharmasist*

ONLY THE CHEMIST can tell, and not always the chemist,
What will result from compounding
Fluids or solids.
And who can tell
How men and women will interact
On each other, or what children will result?
There were Benjamin Pantier and his wife,
Good in themselves, but evil toward each other:
He oxygen, she hydrogen,
Their son, a devastating fire.
I Trainor, the druggist, a mixer of chemicals,
Killed while making an experiment,
Lived unwedded.

Content for not married

Daisy Fraser

DID YOU EVER hear of Editor Whedon
Giving to the public treasury any of the money he received
For supporting candidates for office?
Or for writing up the canning factory
To get people to invest?
Or for suppressing the facts about the bank,
When it was rotten and ready to break?
Did you ever hear of the Circuit Judge
Helping anyone except the "Q" railroad,
Or the bankers? Or did Rev. Peet or Rev. Sibley
Give any part of their salary, earned by keeping still,
Or speaking out as the leaders wished them to do,
To the building of the water works?
But I—Daisy Fraser who always passed
Along the streets through rows of nods and smiles,
And coughs and words such as "there she goes."
Never was taken before Justice Arnett
Without contributing ten dollars and costs
To the school fund of Spoon River!

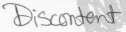

Discontent

Benjamin Fraser

THEIR SPIRITS BEAT upon mine
Like the wings of a thousand butterflies.
I closed my eyes and felt their spirits vibrating.
I closed my eyes, yet I knew when their lashes
Fringed their cheeks from downcast eyes,
And when they turned their heads;
And when their garments clung to them,
Or fell from them, in exquisite draperies.
Their spirits watched my ecstasy
With wide looks of starry unconcern.
Their spirits looked upon my torture;
They drank it as it were the water of life;
With reddened cheeks, brightened eyes,
The rising flame of my soul made their spirits gilt,
Like the wings of a butterfly drifting suddenly into sunlight.
And they cried to me for life, life, life.
But in taking life for myself,
In seizing and crushing their souls,
As a child crushes grapes and drinks
From its palms the purple juice,
I came to this wingless void,
Where neither red, nor gold, nor wine, } Hell?
Nor the rhythm of life is known.

Minerva Jones

I AM MINERVA, the village poetess,
Hooted at, jeered at by the Yahoos of the street
For my heavy body, cock-eye, and rolling walk,
And all the more when "Butch" Weldy
Captured me after a brutal hunt.
He left me to my fate with Doctor Meyers; Abortion
And I sank into death, growing numb from the feet up,
Like one stepping deeper and deeper into a stream of ice.
Will some one go to the village newspaper,
And gather into a book the verses I wrote?—
I thirsted so for love
I hungered so for life![†]

Discontent

"Indignation" Jones — Carpenter

YOU WOULD NOT believe, would you,
That I came from good Welsh stock?
That I was purer blooded than the white trash here?
And of more direct lineage than the New Englanders
And Virginians of Spoon River?
You would not believe that I had been to school
And read some books.
You saw me only as a run-down man,
With matted hair and beard
And ragged clothes.
Sometimes a man's life turns into a cancer
From being bruised and continually bruised,
And swells into a purplish mass,
Like growths on stalks of corn.
Here was I, a carpenter, mired in a bog of life
Into which I walked, thinking it was a meadow,[†]
With a slattern for a wife, and poor Minerva, my daughter,
Whom you tormented and drove to death.
So I crept, crept, like a snail through the days
Of my life.
No more you hear my footsteps in the morning,
Resounding on the hollow sidewalk
Going to the grocery store for a little corn meal
And a nickel's worth of bacon.

Doctor Meyers — ~~Abortionest~~

NO OTHER MAN, unless it was Doc Hill,
Did more for people in this town than I.
And all the weak, the halt, the improvident
And those who could not pay flocked to me.
I was good-hearted, easy Doctor Meyers.
I was healthy, happy, in comfortable fortune,
Blessed with a congenial mate, my children raised,
All wedded, doing well in the world.
And then one night, Minerva, the poetess,
Came to me in her trouble, crying.
I tried to help her out—she died—[†] *she wanted the Abortion*
They indicted me, the newspapers disgraced me,
My wife perished of a broken heart.
And pneumonia finished me.

Mrs. Meyers

HE PROTESTED ALL his life long
The newspapers lied about him villainously;
That he was not at fault for Minerva's fall,
But only tried to help her.
Poor soul so sunk in sin he could not see
That even trying to help her, as he called it,
He had broken the law human and divine.[†]
Passers by, an ancient admonition to you:
If your ways would be ways of pleasantness,
And all your pathways peace,
Love God and keep his commandments.[†]

"Butch" Weldy – MASON

AFTER I GOT religion and steadied down
They gave me a job in the canning works,
And every morning I had to fill
The tank in the yard with gasoline,
That fed the blow-fires in the sheds
To heat the soldering irons.
And I mounted a rickety ladder to do it,
Carrying buckets full of the stuff.
One morning, as I stood there pouring,
The air grew still and seemed to heave,
And I shot up as the tank exploded,
And down I came with both legs broken,
And my eyes burned crisp as a couple of eggs.
For someone left a blow-fire going,
And something sucked the flame in the tank.
The Circuit Judge said whoever did it
Was a fellow-servant of mine, and so
Old Rhodes' son didn't have to pay me.
And I sat on the witness stand as blind
As Jack the Fiddler, saying over and over,
"I didn't know him at all."

Knowlt Hoheimer

I WAS THE first fruits of the battle of Missionary Ridge.[†]
When I felt the bullet enter my heart
I wished I had staid[†] at home and gone to jail
For stealing the hogs of Curl Trenary,
Instead of running away and joining the army.
Rather a thousand times the county jail
Than to lie under this marble figure with wings,
And this granite pedestal
Bearing the words, "*Pro Patria*."[†]
What do they mean, anyway?

Lydia Puckett

KNOWLT HOHEIMER RAN away to the war
The day before Curl Trenary
Swore out a warrant through Justice Arnett
For stealing hogs.
But that's not the reason he turned a soldier.
He caught me running with Lucius Atherton.
We quarreled and I told him never again
To cross my path.
Then he stole the hogs and went to the war—
Back of every soldier is a woman.[†]

Anger, Revenge

Frank Drummer

OUT OF A cell into this darkened space—
The end at twenty-five!
My tongue could not speak what stirred within me,
And the village thought me a fool.
Yet at the start there was a clear vision,
A high and urgent purpose in my soul
Which drove me on trying to memorize
The Encyclopædia Britannica!

Hare Drummer

Do THE BOYS and girls still go to Siever's
For cider, after school, in late September?
Or gather hazel nuts among the thickets
On Aaron Hatfield's farm when the frosts begin?
For many times with the laughing girls and boys
Played I along the road and over the hills
When the sun was low and the air was cool,
Stopping to club the walnut tree
Standing leafless against a flaming west.
Now, the smell of the autumn smoke,
And the dropping acorns,
And the echoes about the vales
Bring dreams of life. They hover over me.
They question me:
Where are those laughing comrades?
How many are with me, how many
In the old orchards along the way to Siever's,
And in the woods that overlook
The quiet water?

Conrad Siever

NOT IN THAT wasted garden
Where bodies are drawn into grass
That feeds no flocks, and into evergreens
That bear no fruit—
There where along the shaded walks
Vain sighs are heard,
And vainer dreams are dreamed
Of close communion with departed souls—
But here under the apple tree
I loved and watched and pruned
With gnarled hands
In the long, long years;
Here under the roots of this northern-spy[†]
To move in the chemic change and circle of life,
Into the soil and into the flesh of the tree,
And into the living epitaphs
Of redder apples!

Doc Hill

I WENT UP and down the streets
Here and there by day and night,
Through all hours of the night caring for the poor who were sick.
Do you know why?
My wife hated me, my son went to the dogs.
And I turned to the people and poured out my love to them.
Sweet it was to see the crowds about the lawns on the day of my funeral,
And hear them murmur their love and sorrow.
But oh, dear God, my soul trembled—scarcely able
To hold to the railing of the new life
When I saw Em Stanton behind the oak tree
At the grave,
Hiding herself, and her grief!

Regret
Love Unrequited

Andy The Night-Watch

Walkin

IN MY SPANISH cloak,
And old slouch hat,
And overshoes of felt,
And Tyke, my faithful dog,
And my knotted hickory cane,
I slipped about with a bull's-eye lantern
From door to door on the square,
As the midnight stars wheeled round,
And the bell in the steeple murmured
From the blowing of the wind;
And the weary steps of old Doc Hill
Sounded like one who walks in sleep,
And a far-off rooster crew.
And now another is watching Spoon River
As others watched before me.
And here we lie, Doc Hill and I
Where none breaks through and steals,
And no eye needs to guard.

Sarah Brown

MAURICE, WEEP NOT, I am not here under this pine tree.
The balmy air of spring whispers through the sweet grass,
The stars sparkle, the whippoorwill calls,
But thou grievest, while my soul lies rapturous
In the blest Nirvana† of eternal light!
Go to the good heart that is my husband,
Who broods upon what he calls our guilty love:—
Tell him that my love for you, no less than my love for him,
Wrought out my destiny—that through the flesh
I won spirit, and through spirit, peace.
There is no marriage in heaven
But there is love.

Regret Content

Percy Bysshe Shelley †

MY FATHER WHO owned the wagon-shop
And grew rich shoeing horses
Sent me to the University of Montreal.
I learned nothing and returned home,
Roaming the fields with Bert Kessler,
Hunting quail and snipe.
At Thompson's Lake the trigger of my gun
Caught in the side of the boat
And a great hole was shot through my heart.
Over me a fond father erected this marble shaft,
On which stands the figure of a woman
Carved by an Italian artist.
They say the ashes of my namesake
Were scattered near the pyramid of Caius Cestius†
Somewhere near Rome.

Flossie Cabanis

FROM BINDLE'S OPERA house in the village
To Broadway is a great step.
But I tried to take it, my ambition fired
When sixteen years of age,
Seeing "East Lynne,"† played here in the village
By Ralph Barrett, the coming
Romantic actor, who enthralled my soul.
True, I trailed back home, a broken failure,
When Ralph disappeared in New York,
Leaving me alone in the city—
But life broke him also.
In all this place of silence
There are no kindred spirits.
How I wish Duse† could stand amid the pathos
Of these quiet fields
And read these words.

Julia Miller

WE QUARRELED THAT morning,
For he was sixty-five, and I was thirty,
And I was nervous and heavy with the child
Whose birth I dreaded.
I thought over the last letter written me
By that estranged young soul
Whose betrayal of me I had concealed
By marrying the old man.
Then I took morphine† and sat down to read.
Across the blackness that came over my eyes
I see the flickering light of these words even now:
"And Jesus said unto him, Verily
I say unto thee, To-day thou shalt
Be with me in paradise."

Misses unborn child
Adultary, Abortion

Johnnie Sayre

FATHER, THOU CANST never know
The anguish that smote my heart
For my disobedience, the moment I felt
The remorseless wheel of the engine
Sink into the crying flesh of my leg.
As they carried me to the home of widow Morris
I could see the school-house in the valley
To which I played truant to steal rides upon the trains.
I prayed to live until I could ask your forgiveness—
And then your tears, your broken words of comfort!
From the solace of that hour I have gained infinite happiness.
Thou wert wise to chisel for me:
"Taken from the evil to come."

Content

Charlie French

DID YOU EVER find out
Which one of the O'Brien boys it was
Who snapped the toy pistol against my hand?
There when the flags were red and white
In the breeze and "Bucky" Estil
Was firing the cannon brought to Spoon River
From Vicksburg[†] by Captain Harris;
And the lemonade stands were running
And the band was playing,
To have it all spoiled
By a piece of a cap shot under the skin of my hand,
And the boys all crowding about me saying:
"You'll die of lock-jaw, Charlie, sure."
Oh, dear! oh, dear!
What chum of mine could have done it?

? Discontent

Zenas Witt

I WAS SIXTEEN, and I had the most terrible dreams,
And specks before my eyes, and nervous weakness.
And I couldn't remember the books I read,
Like Frank Drummer who memorized page after page.
And my back was weak, and I worried and worried,
And I was embarrassed and stammered my lessons,
And when I stood up to recite I'd forget
Everything that I had studied.
Well, I saw Dr. Weese's advertisement,
And there I read everything in print,
Just as if he had known me;
And about the dreams which I couldn't help.
So I knew I was marked for an early grave.
And I worried until I had a cough,
And then the dreams stopped.
And then I slept the sleep without dreams
Here on the hill by the river.

Doc Weese's Serum - Killed him

Theodore the Poet †

As A BOY, Theodore, you sat for long hours
On the shore of the turbid Spoon
With deep-set eye staring at the door of the craw-fish's burrow,
Waiting for him to appear, pushing ahead,
First his waving antennæ, like straws of hay,
And soon his body, colored like soap-stone,
Gemmed with eyes of jet.
And you wondered in a trance of thought
What he knew, what he desired, and why he lived at all.
But later your vision watched for men and women
Hiding in burrows of fate amid great cities,
Looking for the souls of them to come out,
So that you could see
How they lived, and for what,
And why they kept crawling so busily
Along the sandy way where water fails
As the summer wanes.

The Town Marshal

THE PROHIBITIONISTS† MADE me Town Marshal
When the saloons were voted out,
Because when I was a drinking man,
Before I joined the church, I killed a Swede
At the saw-mill near Maple Grove.
And they wanted a terrible man,
Grim, righteous, strong, courageous,
And a hater of saloons and drinkers,
To keep law and order in the village.
And they presented me with a loaded cane
With which I struck Jack McGuire
Before he drew the gun with which he killed me.
The Prohibitionists spent their money in vain
To hang him, for in a dream
I appeared to one of the twelve jurymen
And told him the whole secret story.
Fourteen years were enough for killing me.

Jack McGuire

THEY WOULD HAVE lynched me
Had I not been secretly hurried away
To the jail at Peoria.[†]
And yet I was going peacefully home,
Carrying my jug, a little drunk,
When Logan, the marshal, halted me
Called me a drunken hound and shook me,
And, when I cursed him for it, struck me
With that Prohibition loaded cane—
All this before I shot him.
They would have hanged me except for this:
My lawyer, Kinsey Keene, was helping to land
Old Thomas Rhodes for wrecking the bank,
And the judge was a friend of Rhodes
And wanted him to escape,
And Kinsey offered to quit on Rhodes
For fourteen years for me.
And the bargain was made. I served my time
And learned to read and write.[†]

Dorcas[†] Gustine

I WAS NOT beloved of the villagers,
But all because I spoke my mind,
And met those who transgressed against me
With plain remonstrance, hiding nor nurturing
Nor secret griefs nor grudges.
That act of the Spartan boy[†] is greatly praised,
Who hid the wolf under his cloak,
Letting it devour him, uncomplainingly.
It is braver, I think, to snatch the wolf forth
And fight him openly, even in the street,
Amid dust and howls of pain.
The tongue may be an unruly member—
But silence poisons the soul.[†]
Berate me who will—I am content.

Nicholas Bindle

WERE YOU NOT ashamed, fellow citizens,
When my estate was probated[†] and everyone knew
How small a fortune I left?—
You who hounded me in life,
To give, give, give to the churches, to the poor,
To the village!—me who had already given much.
And think you not I did not know
That the pipe-organ, which I gave to the church,
Played its christening songs when Deacon Rhodes,
Who broke the bank and all but ruined me,
Worshipped for the first time after his acquittal?

Jacob Goodpasture

WHEN FORT SUMTER[†] fell and the war came
I cried out in bitterness of soul:
"O glorious republic now no more!"
When they buried my soldier son
To the call of trumpets and the sound of drums
My heart broke beneath the weight
Of eighty years, and I cried:
"Oh, son who died in a cause unjust!
In the strife of Freedom slain!"
And I crept here under the grass.
And now from the battlements of time, behold:
Thrice thirty million souls being bound together[†]
In the love of larger truth,
Rapt in the expectation of the birth
Of a new Beauty,
Sprung from Brotherhood and Wisdom.
I with eyes of spirit see the Transfiguration[†]
Before you see it.
But ye infinite brood of golden eagles[†] nesting ever higher,
Wheeling ever higher, the sun-light wooing
Of lofty places of Thought,
Forgive the blindness of the departed owl.[†]

Harold Arnett

I LEANED AGAINST the mantel, sick, sick,
Thinking of my failure, looking into the abysm,
Weak from the noon-day heat.
A church bell sounded mournfully far away,
I heard the cry of a baby,
And the coughing of John Yarnell,
Bed-ridden, feverish, feverish, dying,
Then the violent voice of my wife:
"Watch out, the potatoes are burning!"
I smelled them...then there was irresistible disgust.
I pulled the trigger...blackness...light...
Unspeakable regret...fumbling for the world again.
Too late! Thus I came here,
With lungs for breathing...one cannot breathe here with lungs,
Though one must breathe...Of what use is it
To rid one's self of the world,
When no soul may ever escape the eternal destiny of life?

Suicide

Margaret Fuller† Slack

I WOULD HAVE been as great as George Eliot†
But for an untoward fate.
For look at the photograph of me made by Peniwit,
Chin resting on hand, and deep-set eyes—
Gray, too, and far-searching.
But there was the old, old problem:
Should it be celibacy, matrimony or unchastity?
Then John Slack, the rich druggist, wooed me,
Luring me with the promise of leisure for my novel,
And I married him, giving birth to eight children,
And had no time to write.
It was all over with me, anyway,
When I ran the needle in my hand
While washing the baby's things,
And died from lock-jaw, an ironical death.
Hear me, ambitious souls,
Sex is the curse of life!†

Regret

George Trimble

DO YOU REMEMBER when I stood on the steps
Of the Court House and talked free-silver,
And the single-tax of Henry George?[†]
Then do you remember that, when the Peerless Leader[†]
Lost the first battle, I began to talk prohibition,
And became active in the church?
That was due to my wife,
Who pictured to me my destruction
If I did not prove my morality to the people.
Well, she ruined me:[†]
For the radicals[†] grew suspicious of me,
And the conservatives[†] were never sure of me—
And here I lie, unwept of all.

Regret

Dr. Siegrfied Iseman

I SAID WHEN they handed me my diploma,
I said to myself I will be good
And wise and brave and helpful to others;
I said I will carry the Christian creed
Into the practice of medicine!
Somehow the world and the other doctors
Know what's in your heart as soon as you make
This high-souled resolution.
And the way of it is they starve you out.
And no one comes to you but the poor.
And you find too late that being a doctor
Is just a way of making a living.
And when you are poor and have to carry
The Christian creed and wife and children
All on your back, it is too much!
That's why I made the Elixir of Youth,
Which landed me in the jail at Peoria
Branded a swindler and a crook
By the upright Federal Judge!

"Ace"† Shaw

I NEVER SAW any difference
Between playing cards for money
And selling real estate,
Practicing law, banking, or anything else.
For everything is chance.
Nevertheless
Seest thou a man diligent in business?
He shall stand before Kings!†

Lois Spears

HERE LIES THE body of Lois Spears,
Born Lois Fluke,† daughter of Willard Fluke,
Wife of Cyrus Spears,
Mother of Myrtle and Virgil Spears,
Children with clear eyes and sound limbs—
(I was born blind)
I was the happiest of women
As wife, mother and housekeeper,
Caring for my loved ones,
And making my home
A place of order and bounteous hospitality:
For I went about the rooms,
And about the garden
With an instinct as sure as sight,†
As though there were in my finger tips—
Glory to God in the highest.

Justice Arnett

IT IS TRUE, fellow citizens,
That my old docket lying there for years
On a shelf above my head and over
The seat of justice, I say it is true
That docket had an iron rim
Which gashed my baldness when it fell—
(Somehow I think it was shaken loose
By the heave of the air all over town
When the gasoline tank at the canning works
Blew up and burned Butch Weldy)—
But let us argue points in order,
And reason the whole case carefully:
First I concede my head was cut,
But second the frightful thing was this:
The leaves of the docket shot and showered
Around me like a deck of cards
In the hands of a sleight of hand performer.
And up to the end I saw those leaves
Till I said at last, "Those are not leaves,
Why, can't you see they are days and days
And the days and days of seventy years?
And why do you torture me with leaves†
And the little entries on them?

Willard Fluke

MY WIFE LOST her health,
And dwindled until she weighed scarce ninety pounds.
Then that woman, whom the men
Styled Cleopatra,[†] came along.
And we—we married ones
All broke our vows, myself among the rest.
Years passed and one by one
Death claimed them all in some hideous form,
And I was borne along by dreams
Of God's particular grace for me,
And I began to write, write, write, reams on reams
Of the second coming of Christ.
Then Christ came to me and said,
"Go into the church and stand before the congregation
And confess your sin."
But just as I stood up and began to speak
I saw my little girl, who was sitting in the front seat—
My little girl who was born blind![†]
After that, all is blackness![†]

Adultery

Aner Clute

OVER AND OVER they used to ask me,
While buying the wine or the beer,
In Peoria first, and later in Chicago,
Denver, Frisco, New York, wherever I lived,
How I happened to lead the life,
And what was the start of it.
Well, I told them a silk dress,
And a promise of marriage from a rich man—
(It was Lucius Atherton).
But that was not really it at all.
Suppose a boy steals an apple
From the tray at the grocery store,
And they all begin to call him a thief,
The editor, minister, judge, and all the people—
"A thief," "a thief," "a thief," wherever he goes
And he can't get work, and he can't get bread
Without stealing it, why, the boy will steal.
It's the way the people regard the theft of the apple
That makes the boy what he is.[†]

Lucius Atherton

WHEN MY MOUSTACHE curled,
And my hair was black,
And I wore tight trousers
And a diamond stud,
I was an excellent knave of hearts and took many a trick.
But when the gray hairs began to appear—
Lo! a new generation of girls
Laughed at me, not fearing me,
And I had no more exciting adventures
Wherein I was all but shot for a heartless devil,
But only drabby affairs, warmed-over affairs
Of other days and other men.
And time went on until I lived at Mayer's restaurant,
Partaking of short-orders, a gray, untidy,
Toothless, discarded, rural Don Juan…
There is a mighty shade here who sings
Of one named Beatrice;
And I see now that the force that made him great
Drove me to the dregs of life.[†]

Homer Clapp

OFTEN ANER CLUTE at the gate
Refused me the parting kiss,
Saying we should be engaged before that;
And just with a distant clasp of the hand
She bade me good-night, as I brought her home
From the skating rink or the revival.
No sooner did my departing footsteps die away
Than Lucius Atherton,
(So I learned when Aner went to Peoria)
Stole in at her window, or took her riding
Behind his spanking team of bays
Into the country.
The shock of it made me settle down,
And I put all the money I got from my father's estate
Into the canning factory, to get the job
Of head accountant, and lost it all.
And then I knew I was one of Life's fools,
Whom only death would treat as the equal
Of other men, making me feel like a man.[†]

Possible cause of explosion

Deacon Taylor

I BELONGED TO the church,
And to the party of prohibition;
And the villagers thought I died of eating watermelon.
In truth I had cirrhosis of the liver,
For every noon for thirty years,
I slipped behind the prescription partition
In Trainor's drug store
And poured a generous drink
From the bottle marked "*Spiritus frumenti.*"[†]

Sam Hookey

I RAN AWAY from home with the circus,
Having fallen in love with Mademoiselle Estralada,
The lion tamer.
One time, having starved the lions
For more than a day,
I entered the cage and began to beat Brutus
And Leo and Gypsy.
Whereupon Brutus sprang upon me,
And killed me.[†]
On entering these regions
I met a shadow who cursed me,
And said it served me right…
It was Robespierre![†]

Cooney Potter

I INHERITED FORTY acres from my Father
And, by working my wife, my two sons and two daughters
From dawn to dusk, I acquired
A thousand acres. But not content,
Wishing to own two thousand acres,
I bustled through the years with axe and plow,
Toiling, denying myself, my wife, my sons, my daughters.
Squire Higbee wrongs me to say
That I died from smoking Red Eagle cigars.
Eating hot pie and gulping coffee
During the scorching hours of harvest time
Brought me here ere I had reached my sixtieth year.

Fiddler Jones

THE EARTH KEEPS some vibration going
There in your heart, and that is you.
And if the people find you can fiddle,
Why, fiddle you must, for all your life.
What do you see, a harvest of clover?
Or a meadow to walk through to the river?
The wind's in the corn; you rub your hands
For beeves hereafter ready for market;
Or else you hear the rustle of skirts
Like the girls when dancing at Little Grove.
To Cooney Potter a pillar of dust
Or whirling leaves meant ruinous drouth;
They looked to me like Red-Head Sammy
Stepping it off, to "Toor-a-Loor."†
How could I till my forty acres
Not to speak of getting more,
With a medley of horns, bassoons and piccolos
Stirred in my brain by crows and robins
And the creak of a wind-mill—only these?
And I never started to plow in my life
That some one did not stop in the road
And take me away to a dance or picnic.
I ended up with forty acres;
I ended up with a broken fiddle—
And a broken laugh, and a thousand memories,
And not a single regret.†

Content

Nellie Clark

I WAS ONLY eight years old;
And before I grew up and knew what it meant
I had no words for it, except
That I was frightened and told my Mother;
And that my Father got a pistol
And would have killed Charlie, who was a big boy,
Fifteen years old, except for his Mother.
Nevertheless the story clung to me.
But the man who married me, a widower of thirty-five,
Was a newcomer and never heard it
Till two years after we were married.
Then he considered himself cheated,
And the village agreed that I was not really a virgin.
Well, he deserted me,[†] and I died
The following winter.

Louise Smith

HERBERT BROKE OUR engagement of eight years
When Annabelle returned to the village
From the Seminary, ah me!
If I had let my love for him alone
It might have grown into a beautiful sorrow—
Who knows?—filling my life with healing fragrance.
But I tortured it, I poisoned it,
I blinded its eyes, and it became hatred—
Deadly ivy instead of clematis.
And my soul fell from its support,
Its tendrils tangled in decay.
Do not let the will play gardener to your soul[†]
Unless you are sure
It is wiser than your soul's nature.

Herbert Marshall

ALL YOUR SORROW, Louise, and hatred of me
Sprang from your delusion that it was wantonness
Of spirit and contempt of your soul's rights
Which made me turn to Annabelle and forsake you.
You really grew to hate me for love of me,
Because I was your soul's happiness,
Formed and tempered
To solve your life for you, and would not.
But you were my misery. If you had been
My happiness would I not have clung to you?
This is life's sorrow:
That one can be happy only where two are;
And that our hearts are drawn to stars
Which want us not.

George Gray

I HAVE STUDIED many times
The marble which was chiseled for me—
A boat with a furled sail at rest in a harbor.
In truth it pictures not my destination
But my life.
For love was offered me and I shrank from its disillusionment;
Sorrow knocked at my door, but I was afraid;
Ambition called to me, but I dreaded the chances.
Yet all the while I hungered for meaning in my life.
And now I know that we must lift the sail
And catch the winds of destiny
Wherever they drive the boat.
To put meaning in one's life may end in madness,
But life without meaning is the torture
Of restlessness and vague desire—
It is a boat longing for the sea and yet afraid.[†]

Hon. Henry Bennett

IT NEVER CAME into my mind
Until I was ready to die
That Jenny had loved me to death, with malice of heart.
For I was seventy, she was thirty-five,
And I wore myself to a shadow trying to husband
Jenny, rosy Jenny full of the ardor of life.
For all my wisdom and grace of mind
Gave her no delight at all, in very truth,
But ever and anon she spoke of the giant strength
Of Willard Shafer, and of his wonderful feat
Of lifting a traction engine out of the ditch
One time at Georgie Kirby's.
So Jenny inherited my fortune and married Willard—
That mount of brawn! That clownish soul![†]

Griffy the Cooper

THE COOPER SHOULD know about tubs.
But I learned about life as well,
And you who loiter around these graves
Think you know life.
You think your eye sweeps about a wide horizon, perhaps,
In truth you are only looking around the interior of your tub.
You cannot lift yourself to its rim
And see the outer world of things,
And at the same time see yourself.
You are submerged in the tub of yourself—
Taboos and rules and appearances,
Are the staves of your tub.
Break them and dispel the witchcraft
Of thinking your tub is life!
And that you know life!

Sersmith the Dentist

Do YOU THINK that odes and sermons,
And the ringing of church bells,
And the blood of old men and young men,
Martyred for the truth they saw
With eyes made bright by faith in God,
Accomplished the world's great reformations?
Do you think that the Battle Hymn of the Republic†
Would have been heard if the chattel slave
Had crowned the dominant dollar,
In spite of Whitney's cotton gin,†
And steam and rolling mills and iron
And telegraphs and white free labor?
Do you think that Daisy Fraser
Had been put out and driven out
If the canning works had never needed
Her little house and lot?
Or do you think the poker room
Of Johnnie Taylor, and Burchard's bar
Had been closed up if the money lost
And spent for beer had not been turned,
By closing them, to Thomas Rhodes
For larger sales of shoes and blankets,
And children's cloaks and gold-oak cradles?
Why, a moral truth is a hollow tooth
Which must be propped with gold.

A. D. Blood

IF YOU IN the village think that my work was a good one,
Who closed the saloons and stopped all playing at cards,
And haled old Daisy Fraser before Justice Arnett,
In many a crusade to purge the people of sin;
Why do you let the milliner's daughter Dora,
And the worthless son of Benjamin Pantier
Nightly make my grave their unholy pillow?†

Robert Southey† Burke

I SPENT MY money trying to elect you Mayor
A.D. Blood.
I lavished my admiration upon you,
You were to my mind the almost perfect man.
You devoured my personality,
And the idealism of my youth,
And the strength of a high-souled fealty.
And all my hopes for the world,
And all my beliefs in Truth,
Were smelted up in the blinding heat
Of my devotion to you,
And molded into your image.
And the when I found what you were:
That your soul was small
And your words were false
As your blue-white porcelain teeth,
And your cuffs of celluloid,
I hated the love I had for you,
I hated myself, I hated you
For my wasted soul, and wasted youth.
And I say to all, beware of ideals,
Beware of giving your love away
To any man alive.

Dora Williams

WHEN REUBEN PANTIER ran away and threw me
I went to Springfield. There I met a lush,
Whose father just deceased left him a fortune.
He married me when drunk. My life was wretched.
A year passed and one day they found him dead.
That made me rich. I moved on to Chicago.
After a time met Tyler Rountree, villain.
I moved on to New York. A gray-haired magnate
Went mad about me—so another fortune.
He died one night right in my arms, you know.
(I saw his purple face for years thereafter.)
There was almost a scandal. I moved on,
This time to Paris. I was now a woman,
Insidious, subtle, versed in the world and rich.
My sweet apartment near the Champs Élysées[†]
Became a center for all sorts of people,
Musicians, poets, dandies, artists, nobles,
Where we spoke French and German, Italian, English.
I wed Count Navigato, native of Genoa.
We went to Rome. He poisoned me, I think.
Now in the Campo Santo[†] overlooking
The sea where young Columbus[†] dreamed new worlds,
See what they chiseled: "*Contessa Navigato
Implora eterna quiete.*"[†]

Mrs. Williams

I WAS THE milliner
Talked about, lied about,
Mother of Dora,
Whose strange disappearance
Was charged to her rearing.[†]
My eye quick to beauty
Saw much beside ribbons
And buckles and feathers
And leghorns and felts,
To set off sweet faces,
And dark hair and gold.
One thing I will tell you
And one I will ask:
The stealers of husbands
Wear powder and trinkets,
And fashionable hats.
Wives, wear them yourselves.
Hats may make divorces—
They also prevent them.
Well now, let me ask you:
If all of the children, born here in Spoon River
Had been reared by the County, somewhere on a farm;
And the fathers and mothers had been given their freedom
To live and enjoy, change mates if they wished,
Do you think that Spoon River
Had been any the worse?

William and Emily

THERE IS SOMETHING about Death
Like love itself!
If with some one with whom you have known passion,
And the glow of youthful love,
You also, after years of life
Together, feel the sinking of the fire
And thus fade away together,
Gradually, faintly, delicately,
As it were in each other's arms,
Passing from the familiar room—
That is a power of unison between souls
Like love itself![†]

The Circuit Judge

TAKE NOTE, PASSERS-BY, of the sharp erosions
Eaten in my head-stone by the wind and rain—
Almost as if an intangible Nemesis[†] or hatred
Were marking scores against me,
But to destroy, and not preserve, my memory.
I in life was the Circuit Judge, a maker of notches,
Deciding cases on the points the lawyers scored,
Not on the right of the matter.
O wind and rain, leave my head-stone alone
For worse than the anger of the wronged,
The curses of the poor,
Was to lie speechless, yet with vision clear,
Seeing that even Hod Putt, the murderer,
Hanged by my sentence,
Was innocent in soul compared with me.

Blind Jack

I HAD FIDDLED all day at the county fair.
But driving home "Butch" Weldy and Jack McGuire,
Who were roaring full, made me fiddle and fiddle
To the song of *Susie Skinner*, while whipping the horses
Till they ran away.
Blind as I was, I tried to get out
As the carriage fell in the ditch,
And was caught in the wheels and killed.
There's a blind man here with a brow
As big and white as a cloud.
And all we fiddlers, from highest to lowest,
Writers of music and tellers of stories,
Sit at his feet,
And hear him sing of the fall of Troy.[†]

John Horace Burleson

I WON THE prize essay at school
Here in the village,
And published a novel before I was twenty-five.
I went to the city for themes and to enrich my art;[†]
There married the banker's daughter,
And later became president of the bank—
Always looking forward to some leisure
To write an epic novel of the war.
Meanwhile friend of the great, and lover of letters,
And host to Matthew Arnold[†] and to Emerson.[†]
An after dinner speaker, writing essays
For local clubs. At last brought here—
My boyhood home, you know—
Not even a little tablet in Chicago
To keep my name alive.
How great it is to write the single line:
"Roll on, thou deep and dark blue Ocean, roll!"[†]

Nancy Knapp

WELL, DON'T YOU see this was the way of it:
We bought the farm with what he inherited,
And his brothers and sisters accused him of poisoning
His father's mind against the rest of them.
And we never had any peace with our treasure.
The murrain took the cattle, and the crops failed.
And lightning struck the granary.[†]
So we mortgaged the farm to keep going.
And he grew silent and was worried all the time.
Then some of the neighbors refused to speak to us,
And took sides with his brothers and sisters.
And I had no place to turn, as one may say to himself,
At an earlier time in life; "No matter,
So and so is my friend, or I can shake this off
With a little trip to Decatur."[†]
Then the dreadfullest smells infested the rooms.
So I set fire to the beds and the old witch-house
Went up in a roar of flame,
As I danced in the yard with waving arms,
While he wept like a freezing steer.

Barry Holden

THE VERY FALL my sister Nancy Knapp
Set fire to the house
They were trying Dr. Duval
For the murder of Zora Clemens,
And I sat in the court two weeks
Listening to every witness.
It was clear he had got her in a family way;
And to let the child be born
Would not do.
Well, how about me with eight children,
And one coming, and the farm
Mortgaged to Thomas Rhodes?
And when I got home that night,
(After listening to the story of the buggy ride,
And the finding of Zora in the ditch,)
The first thing I saw, right there by the steps,
Where the boys had hacked for angle worms,
Was the hatchet!
And just as I entered there was my wife,
Standing before me, big with child.
She started the talk of the mortgaged farm,
And I killed her.†

State's Attorney Fallas

I, THE SCOURGE-WIELDER, balance-wrecker,
Smiter with whips and swords;
I, hater of the breakers of the law;
I, legalist, inexorable and bitter,
Driving the jury to hang the madman, Barry Holden,
Was made as one dead by light too bright for eyes,
And woke to face a Truth with bloody brow:
Steel forceps fumbled by a doctor's hand
Against my boy's head as he entered life
Made him an idiot.
I turned to books of science
To care for him.
That's how the world of those whose minds are sick
Became my work in life, and all my world.
Poor ruined boy! You were, at last, the potter
And I and all my deeds of charity
The vessels of your hand.

Wendell P. Bloyd

THEY FIRST CHARGED me with disorderly conduct,
There being no statute on blasphemy.
Later they locked me up as insane
Where I was beaten to death by a Catholic guard.
My offense was this:
I said God lied to Adam, and destined him
To lead the life of a fool,
Ignorant that there is evil in the world as well as good.
And when Adam outwitted God by eating the apple
And saw through the lie,
God drove him out of Eden to keep him from taking
The fruit of immortal life.
For Christ's sake, you sensible people,
Here's what God Himself says about it in the book of Genesis:
"And the Lord God said, behold the man
Is become as one of us" (a little envy, you see),
"To know good and evil" (The all-is-good lie exposed):
"And now lest he put forth his hand and take
Also of the tree of life and eat, and live forever:
Therefore the Lord God sent Him forth from the garden of Eden."
(The reason I believe God crucified His Own Son
To get out of the wretched tangle is, because it sounds just like Him.)

Francis Turner

I COULD NOT run or play
In boyhood.
In manhood I could only sip the cup,
Not drink—
For scarlet-fever left my heart diseased.
Yet I lie here
Soothed by a secret none but Mary knows:
There is a garden of acacia,
Catalpa trees, and arbors sweet with vines—
There on that afternoon in June
By Mary's side—
Kissing her with my soul upon my lips
It suddenly took flight.

Franklin Jones

IF I COULD have lived another year
I could have finished my flying machine,
And become rich and famous.
Hence it is fitting the workman
Who tried to chisel a dove for me
Made it look more like a chicken.[†]
For what is it all but being hatched,
And running about the yard,
To the day of the block?
Save that a man has an angel's brain,
And sees the ax from the first![†]

John M. Church [†]

I WAS ATTORNEY for the "Q"
And the Indemnity Company which insured
The owners of the mine.
I pulled the wires with judge and jury,
And the upper courts, to beat the claims
Of the crippled, the widow and orphan,
And made a fortune thereat.
The bar association sang my praises
In a high-flown resolution.
And the floral tributes were many—
But the rats devoured my heart
And a snake made a nest in my skull![†]

Russian Sonia

I, BORN IN Weimar[†]
Of a mother who was French
And German father, a most learned professor,
Orphaned at fourteen years,
Became a dancer, known as Russian Sonia,
All up and down the boulevards of Paris,
Mistress betimes of sundry dukes and counts,
And later of poor artists and of poets.
At forty years, *passée*,[†] I sought New York
And met old Patrick Hummer on the boat,
Red-faced and hale, though turned his sixtieth year,
Returning after having sold a ship-load
Of cattle in the German city, Hamburg.
He brought me to Spoon River and we lived here
For twenty years—they thought that we were married!
This oak tree near me is the favorite haunt
Of blue jays chattering, chattering all the day.
And why not? for my very dust is laughing
For thinking of the humorous thing called life.

Isa Nutter

Doc Meyers said I had satyriasis,
And Doc Hill called it leucæmia—
But I know what brought me here:
I was sixty-four but strong as a man
Of thirty-five or forty.
And it wasn't writing a letter a day,
And it wasn't late hours seven nights a week,
And it wasn't the strain of thinking of Minnie,
And it wasn't fear or a jealous dread,
Or the endless task of trying to fathom
Her wonderful mind, or sympathy
For the wretched life she led
With her first and second husband—
It was none of these that laid me low—
But the clamor of daughters and threats of sons,
And the sneers and curses of all my kin
Right up to the day I sneaked to Peoria[†]
And married Minnie in spite of them—
And why do you wonder my will was made
For the best and purest of women?

Barney Hainsfeather

If the excursion train to Peoria
Had just been wrecked, I might have escaped with my life—
Certainly I should have escaped this place.
But as it was burned as well, they mistook me
For John Allen who was sent to the Hebrew Cemetery
At Chicago,
And John for me, so I lie here.
It was bad enough to run a clothing store in this town,
But to be buried here—ach![†]

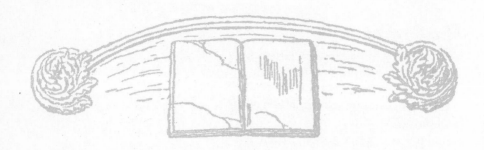

Petit, the Poet

Petit, the Poet

SEEDS IN A dry pod, tick, tick, tick,
Tick, tick, tick, like mites in a quarrel—
Faint iambics that the full breeze wakens—
But the pine tree makes a symphony thereof.
Triolets, villanelles, rondels, rondeaus,
Ballades by the score with the same old thought:
The snows and the roses of yesterday are vanished;
And what is love but a rose that fades?
Life all around me here in the village:
Tragedy, comedy, valor and truth,
Courage, constancy, heroism, failure—
All in the loom, and oh what patterns!
Woodlands, meadows, streams and rivers—
Blind to all of it all my life long.
Triolets, villanelles, rondels, rondeaus,
Seeds in a dry pod, tick, tick, tick,
Tick, tick, tick, what little iambics,
While Homer and Whitman roared in the pines?

Pauline Barrett

ALMOST THE SHELL of a woman after the surgeon's knife!
And almost a year to creep back into strength,
Till the dawn of our wedding decennial
Found me my seeming self again.
We walked the forest together,
By a path of soundless moss and turf.
But I could not look in your eyes,
And you could not look in my eyes,
For such sorrow was ours—the beginning of gray in your hair,
And I but a shell of myself.
And what did we talk of?—sky and water,
Anything, 'most, to hide our thoughts.
And then your gift of wild roses,
Set on the table to grace our dinner.
Poor heart, how bravely you struggled
To imagine and live a remembered rapture!
Then my spirit drooped as the night came on,
And you left me alone in my room for a while,
As you did when I was a bride, poor heart.
And I looked in the mirror and something said:
"One should be all dead when one is half-dead—
Nor ever mock life, nor ever cheat love."
And I did it looking there in the mirror—
Dear, have you ever understood?

Mrs. Charles Bliss

REVEREND WILEY ADVISED me not to divorce him
For the sake of the children,
And Judge Somers advised him the same.
So we stuck to the end of the path.
But two of the children thought he was right,
And two of the children thought I was right.
And the two who sided with him blamed me,
And the two who sided with me blamed him,
And they grieved for the one they sided with.
And all were torn with the guilt of judging,
And tortured in soul because they could not admire
Equally him and me.
Now every gardener knows that plants grown in cellars
Or under stones are twisted and yellow and weak.
And no mother would let her baby suck
Diseased milk from her breast.
Yet preachers and judges advise the raising of souls
Where there is no sunlight, but only twilight,
No warmth, but only dampness and cold—
Preachers and judges!

Mrs. George Reece

TO THIS GENERATION I would say:
Memorize some bit of verse of truth or beauty.
It may serve a turn in your life.
My husband had nothing to do
With the fall of the bank—he was only cashier.
The wreck was due to the president, Thomas Rhodes,
And his vain, unscrupulous son.
Yet my husband was sent to prison,
And I was left with the children,
To feed and clothe and school them.
And I did it, and sent them forth
Into the world all clean and strong,
And all through the wisdom of Pope, the poet:
"Act well your part, there all the honor lies."[†]

Rev. Lemuel Wiley

I PREACHED FOUR thousand sermons,
I conducted forty revivals,
And baptized many converts.
Yet no deed of mine
Shines brighter in the memory of the world,
And none is treasured more by me:
Look how I saved the Blisses from divorce,[†]
And kept the children free from that disgrace,
To grow up into moral men and women,
Happy themselves, a credit to the village.

Thomas Ross, Jr.

THIS I SAW with my own eyes:
A cliff-swallow
Made her nest in a hole of the high clay-bank
There near Miller's Ford.
But no sooner were the young hatched
Than a snake crawled up to the nest
To devour the brood.
Then the mother swallow with swift flutterings
And shrill cries
Fought at the snake,
Blinding him with the beat of her wings,
Until he, wriggling and rearing his head,
Fell backward down the bank
Into Spoon River and was drowned.
Scarcely an hour passed
Until a shrike
Impaled the mother swallow on a thorn.
As for myself I overcame my lower nature
Only to be destroyed by my brother's ambition.[†]

Rev. Abner Peet

I HAD NO objection at all
To selling my household effects at auction
On the village square.
It gave my beloved flock the chance
To get something which had belonged to me
For a memorial.
But that trunk which was struck off
To Burchard, the grog-keeper!
Did you know it contained the manuscripts
Of a lifetime of sermons?
And he burned them as waste paper.†

Jefferson Howard

MY VALIANT FIGHT! For I call it valiant,
With my father's beliefs from old Virginia:
Hating slavery, but no less war.
I, full of spirit, audacity, courage
Thrown into life here in Spoon River,
With its dominant forces drawn from New England,
Republicans, Calvinists,† merchants, bankers,
Hating me, yet fearing my arm.
With wife and children heavy to carry—
Yet fruits of my very zest of life.
Stealing odd pleasures that cost me prestige,
And reaping evils I had not sown;
Foe of the church with its charnel dankness,
Friend of the human touch of the tavern;
Tangled with fates all alien to me,
Deserted by hands I called my own.
Then just as I felt my giant strength
Short of breath, behold my children
Had wound their lives in stranger gardens—
And I stood alone, as I started alone!
My valiant life! I died on my feet,
Facing the silence—facing the prospect
That no one would know of the fight I made.

Judge Selah Lively

SUPPOSE YOU STOOD just five feet two,
And had worked your way as a grocery clerk,
Studying law by candle light
Until you became an attorney at law?
And then suppose through your diligence,
And regular church attendance,
You became attorney for Thomas Rhodes,
Collecting notes and mortgages,
And representing all the widows
In the Probate Court? And through it all
They jeered at your size, and laughed at your clothes
And your polished boots? And then suppose
You became the County Judge?
And Jefferson Howard and Kinsey Keene,
And Harmon Whitney, and all the giants
Who had sneered at you, were forced to stand
Before the bar and say "Your Honor"—
Well, don't you think it was natural
That I made it hard for them?[†]

Albert Schirding

JONAS KEENE THOUGHT his lot a hard one
Because his children were all failures.
But I know of a fate more trying than that:
It is to be a failure while your children are successes.
For I raised a brood of eagles
Who flew away at last, leaving me
A crow on the abandoned bough.
Then, with the ambition to prefix Honorable to my name,
And thus to win my children's admiration,
I ran for County Superintendent of Schools,
Spending my accumulations to win—and lost.
That fall my daughter received first prize in Paris
For her picture, entitled, "The Old Mill"—
(It was of the water mill before Henry Wilkin put in steam.)
The feeling that I was not worthy of her finished me.

Jonas Keene

WHY DID ALBERT SCHIRDING kill himself
Trying to be County Superintendent of Schools,
Blest as he was with the means of life
And wonderful children, bringing him honor
Ere he was sixty?[†]
If even one of my boys could have run a news-stand,
Or one of my girls could have married a decent man,
I should not have walked in the rain
And jumped into bed with clothes all wet,
Refusing medical aid.

Eugenia Todd

HAVE ANY OF you, passers-by,
Had an old tooth that was an unceasing discomfort?
Or a pain in the side that never quite left you?
Or a malignant growth that grew with time?
So that even in profoundest slumber
There was shadowy consciousness or the phantom of thought
Of the tooth, the side, the growth?
Even so thwarted love, or defeated ambition,
Or a blunder in life which mixed your life
Hopelessly to the end,
Will like a tooth, or a pain in the side,
Float through your dreams in the final sleep
Till perfect freedom from the earth-sphere
Comes to you as one who wakes
Healed and glad in the morning![†]

Yee Bow [†]

THEY GOT ME into the Sunday-school
In Spoon River
And tried to get me to drop Confucius for Jesus.
I could have been no worse off
If I had tried to get them to drop Jesus for Confucius. [†]
For, without any warning, as if it were a prank,
And sneaking up behind me, Harry Wiley,
The minister's son, caved my ribs into my lungs,
With a blow of his fist.
Now I shall never sleep with my ancestors in Pekin, [†]
And no children shall worship at my grave.

Washington McNeely

RICH, HONORED BY my fellow citizens,
The father of many children, born of a noble mother,
All raised there
In the great mansion-house, at the edge of town.
Note the cedar tree on the lawn!
I sent all the boys to Ann Arbor,† all of the girls to Rockford,†
The while my life went on, getting more riches and honors—
Resting under my cedar tree at evening.
The years went on.
I sent the girls to Europe;
I dowered them when married.
I gave the boys money to start in business.
They were strong children, promising as apples
Before the bitten places show.
But John fled the country in disgrace.
Jenny died in child-birth—
I sat under my cedar tree.
Harry killed himself after a debauch,
Susan was divorced—
I sat under my cedar tree.
Paul was invalided from over study,
Mary became a recluse at home for love of a man—
I sat under my cedar tree.
All were gone, or broken-winged or devoured by life—
I sat under my cedar tree.
My mate, the mother of them, was taken—
I sat under my cedar tree,
Till ninety years were tolled.
O maternal Earth, which rocks the fallen leaf to sleep!

Paul McNeely

DEAR JANE! dear winsome Jane!
How you stole in the room (where I lay so ill)
In your nurse's cap and linen cuffs,
And took my hand and said with a smile:
"You are not so ill—you'll soon be well."
And how the liquid thought of your eyes
Sank in my eyes like dew that slips
Into the heart of a flower.
Dear Jane! the whole McNeely fortune
Could not have bought your care of me,
By day and night, and night and day;
Nor paid for your smile, nor the warmth of your soul,
In your little hands laid on my brow.
Jane, till the flame of life went out
In the dark above the disk of night
I longed and hoped to be well again
To pillow my head on your little breasts,
And hold you fast in a clasp of love—
Did my father provide for you when he died,
Jane, dear Jane?

Mary McNeely

PASSER-BY,
To love is to find your own soul
Through the soul of the beloved one.
When the beloved one withdraws itself from your soul
Then you have lost your soul.
It is written: "I have a friend,
But my sorrow has no friend."
Hence my long years of solitude at the home of my father,
Trying to get myself back,
And to turn my sorrow into a supremer self.
But there was my father with his sorrows,
Sitting under the cedar tree,
A picture that sank into my heart at last
Bringing infinite repose.
Oh, ye souls who have made life
Fragrant and white as tube roses
From earth's dark soil,
Eternal peace!†

Daniel M'Cumber

WHEN I WENT to the city, Mary McNeely,
I meant to return for you, yes I did.
But Laura, my landlady's daughter,
Stole into my life somehow, and won me away.
Then after some years whom should I meet
But Georgine Miner from Niles†—a sprout
Of the free love, Fourierist† gardens that flourished
Before the war all over Ohio.
Her dilettante lover had tired of her,
And she turned to me for strength and solace.
She was some kind of a crying thing
One takes in one's arms, and all at once
It slimes your face with its running nose,
And voids its essence all over you;
Then bites your hand and springs away.
And there you stand bleeding and smelling to heaven
Why, Mary McNeely, I was not worthy
To kiss the hem of your robe!†

Georgine Sand Miner

A STEPMOTHER DROVE me from home, embittering me.
A squaw-man, a flaneur and dilettante took my virtue.
For years I was his mistress—no one knew.
I learned from him the parasite cunning
With which I moved with the bluffs, like a flea on a dog.
All the time I was nothing but "very private," with different men.
Then Daniel, the radical, had me for years.
His sister called me his mistress;
And Daniel wrote me: "Shameful word, soiling our beautiful love!"
But my anger coiled, preparing its fangs.   *metaphor*
My Lesbian friend next took a hand.
She hated Daniel's sister.
And Daniel despised her midget husband.
And she saw a chance for a poisonous thrust:
I must complain to the wife of Daniel's pursuit!
But before I did that I begged him to fly to London with me.
"Why not stay in the city just as we have?" he asked.
Then I turned submarine and revenged his repulse
In the arms of my dilettante friend. Then up to the surface,
Bearing the letter that Daniel wrote me
To prove my honor was all intact, showing it to his wife,
My Lesbian friend and everyone.
If Daniel had only shot me dead!
Instead of stripping me naked of lies
A harlot in body and soul!

Thomas Rhodes

VERY WELL, YOU liberals,
And navigators into realms intellectual,
You sailors through heights imaginative,
Blown about by erratic currents, tumbling into air pockets,
You Margaret Fuller Slacks, Petits,
And Tennessee Claflin Shopes—
You found with all your boasted wisdom
How hard at the last it is
To keep the soul from splitting into cellular atoms.
While we, seekers of earth's treasures,
Getters and hoarders of gold,
Are self-contained, compact, harmonized,
Even to the end.

Ida Chicken

AFTER I HAD attended lectures
At our Chautauqua,† and studied French
For twenty years, committing the grammar
Almost by heart,
I thought I'd take a trip to Paris
To give my culture a final polish.
So I went to Peoria for a passport—
(Thomas Rhodes was on the train that morning.)
And there the clerk of the district Court
Made me swear to support and defend
The constitution—yes, even me—
Who couldn't defend or support it at all!
And what do you think? That very morning
The Federal Judge, in the very next room
To the room where I took the oath,
Decided the constitution
Exempted Rhodes from paying taxes
For the water works of Spoon River!

Penniwit, the Artist

I LOST MY patronage in Spoon River
From trying to put my mind in the camera
To catch the soul of the person.
The very best picture I ever took
Was of Judge Somers, attorney at law.
He sat upright and had me pause
Till he got his cross-eye straight.
Then when he was ready he said "all right."
And I yell, "overruled" and his eye turned up.
And I caught him just as he used to look
When saying "l except."

Jim Brown

WHILE I WAS handling Dom Pedro†
I got at the thing that divides the race between men who are
For singing "Turkey in the straw"† or "There is a fountain filled with
blood"†—
(Like Rile Potter used to sing it over at Concord†);
For cards, or for Rev. Peet's lecture on the holy land;
For skipping the light fantastic,† or passing the plate;†
For Pinafore,† or a Sunday school cantata;
For men, or for money;
For the people or against them.
This was it:
Rev. Peet and the Social Purity Club,
Headed by Ben Pantier's wife,
Went to the Village trustees,
And asked them to make me take Dom Pedro
From the barn of Wash McNeely, there at the edge of town,
To a barn outside of the corporation,
On the ground that it corrupted public morals.
Well, Ben Pantier and Fiddler Jones saved the day—
They thought it a slam on colts.

Robert Davidson

I GREW SPIRITUALLY fat living off the souls of men.
If I saw a soul that was strong
I wounded its pride and devoured its strength.
The shelters of friendship knew my cunning
For where I could steal a friend I did so.
And wherever I could enlarge my power
By undermining ambition, I did so,
Thus to make smooth my own.
And to triumph over other souls,
Just to assert and prove my superior strength,
Was with me a delight,
The keen exhilaration of soul gymnastics.
Devouring souls, I should have lived forever.
But their undigested remains bred in me a deadly nephritis,
With fear, restlessness, sinking spirits,
Hatred, suspicion, vision disturbed.
I collapsed at last with a shriek.
Remember the acorn;[†]
It does not devour other acorns.

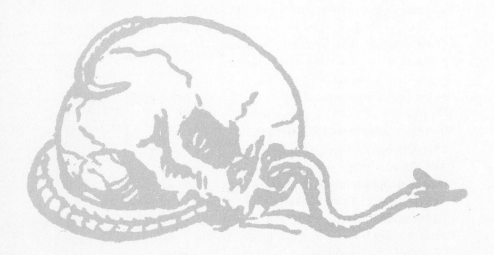

Elsa Wertman

I WAS A peasant girl from Germany,
Blue-eyed, rosy, happy and strong.
And the first place I worked was at Thomas Greene's.
On a summer's day when she was away
He stole into the kitchen and took me
Right in his arms and kissed me on my throat,
I turning my head. Then neither of us
Seemed to know what happened.
And I cried for what would become of me.
And cried and cried as my secret began to show.†
One day Mrs. Greene said she understood,
And would make no trouble for me,
And, being childless, would adopt it.
(He had given her a farm to be still.)
So she hid in the house and sent out rumors,
As if it were going to happen to her.
And all went well and the child was born—They were so kind to me.
Later I married Gus Wertman, and years passed.
But—at political rallies when sitters-by thought I was crying
At the eloquence of Hamilton Greene—
That was not it.
No! I wanted to say:
That's my son! That's my son.

Hamilton Greene

I WAS THE only child of Frances Harris of Virginia
And Thomas Greene of Kentucky,
Of valiant and honorable blood both.
To them I owe all that I became,
Judge, member of Congress, leader in the State.
From my mother I inherited
Vivacity, fancy, language;
From my father will, judgment, logic.
All honor to them
For what service I was to the people!

Ernest Hyde

MY MIND WAS a mirror:
It saw what it saw, it knew what it knew.
In youth my mind was just a mirror
In a rapidly flying car,
Which catches and loses bits of the landscape.
Then in time
Great scratches were made on the mirror,
Letting the outside world come in,
And letting my inner self look out.
For this is the birth of the soul in sorrow,
A birth with gains and losses.
The mind sees the world as a thing apart,
And the soul makes the world at one with itself.
A mirror scratched reflects no image—
And this is the silence of wisdom.

Roger Heston

OH MANY TIMES did Ernest Hyde and I
Argue about the freedom of the will.
My favorite metaphor was Prickett's cow
Roped out to grass, and free you know as far
As the length of the rope.
One day while arguing so, watching the cow
Pull at the rope to get beyond the circle
Which she had eaten bare,
Out came the stake, and tossing up her head,
She ran for us.
"What's that, free-will or what?" said Ernest, running.
I fell just as she gored me to my death.

Amos Sibley

NOT CHARACTER, NOT fortitude, not patience
Were mine, the which the village thought I had
In bearing with my wife, while preaching on,
Doing the work God chose for me.
I loathed her as a termagant, as a wanton.
I knew of her adulteries, every one.
But even so, if I divorced the woman
I must forsake the ministry.
Therefore to do God's work and have it crop,
I bore with her!
So lied I to myself!
So lied I to Spoon River!
Yet I tried lecturing, ran for the legislature,
Canvassed for books, with just the thought in mind:
If I make money thus, I will divorce her.

Mrs. Sibley

THE SECRET OF the stars,—gravitation.
The secret of the earth,—layers of rock.
The secret of the soil,—to receive seed.
The secret of the seed,—the germ.
The secret of man,—the sower.
The secret of woman,—the soil.
My secret: Under a mound that you shall never find.†

Adam Weirauch

I WAS CRUSHED between Altgeld and Armour.
I lost many friends, much time and money
Fighting for Altgeld whom Editor Whedon
Denounced as the candidate of gamblers and anarchists.
Then Armour started to ship dressed meat to Spoon River,
Forcing me to shut down my slaughter-house
And my butcher shop went all to pieces.
The new forces of Altgeld and Armour caught me
At the same time.
I thought it due me, to recoup the money I lost
And to make good the friends that left me,
For the Governor to appoint me Canal Commissioner.
Instead he appointed Whedon of the Spoon River *Argus*,
So I ran for the legislature and was elected.
I said to hell with principle and sold my vote
On Charles T. Yerkes' street-car franchise.
Of course I was one of the fellows they caught.
Who was it, Armour, Altgeld or myself
That ruined me?

Ezra Bartlett

A CHAPLAIN IN the army,
A chaplain in the prisons,
An exhorter in Spoon River,
Drunk with divinity, Spoon River—
Yet bringing poor Eliza Johnson to shame,
And myself to scorn and wretchedness.
But why will you never see that love of women,
And even love of wine,
Are the stimulants by which the soul, hungering for divinity,
Reaches the ecstatic vision[†]
And sees the celestial outposts?[†]
Only after many trials for strength,
Only when all stimulants fail,
Does the aspiring soul
By its own sheer power
Find the divine
By resting upon itself.

Amelia Garrick

YES, HERE I lie close to a stunted rose bush
In a forgotten place near the fence
Where the thickets from Siever's woods
Have crept over, growing sparsely.
And you, you are a leader in New York,
The wife of a noted millionaire,
A name in the society columns,
Beautiful, admired, magnified perhaps
By the mirage of distance.
You have succeeded, I have failed
In the eyes of the world.
You are alive, I am dead.
Yet I know that I vanquished your spirit;
And I know that lying here far from you,
Unheard of among your great friends
In the brilliant world where you move,
I am really the unconquerable power over your life
That robs it of complete triumph.[†]

John Hancock[†] Otis

AS TO DEMOCRACY, fellow citizens,
Are you not prepared to admit
That l, who inherited riches and was to the manner born,[†]
Was second to none in Spoon River
In my devotion to the cause of Liberty?
While my contemporary, Anthony Findlay,
Born in a shanty and beginning life
As a water carrier to the section hands,
Then becoming a section hand when he was grown,
Afterwards foreman of the gang, until he rose
To the superintendency of the railroad,
Living in Chicago,
Was a veritable slave driver,
Grinding the faces of labor,
And a bitter enemy of democracy.
And I say to you, Spoon River,
And to you, O republic,
Beware of the man who rises to power
From one suspender.

Anthony Findlay

BOTH FOR THE country and for the man,
And for a country as well as a man,
'Tis better to be feared than loved.
And if this country would rather part
With the friendship of every nation
Than surrender its wealth,
I say of a man 'tis worse to lose
Money than friends.
And I rend the curtain that hides the soul
Of an ancient aspiration:
When the people clamor for freedom
They really seek for power o'er the strong.
I, Anthony Findlay, rising to greatness
From a humble water carrier,
Until I could say to thousands "Come,"
And say to thousands "Go,"
Affirm that a nation can never be good,
Or achieve the good,
Where the strong and the wise have not the rod
To use on the dull and weak.

John Cabanis

NEITHER SPITE, FELLOW citizens,
Nor forgetfulness of the shiftlessness,
And the lawlessness and waste
Under democracy's rule in Spoon River
Made me desert the party of law and order
And lead the liberal party.
Fellow citizens! I saw as one with second sight
That every man of the millions of men
Who give themselves to Freedom,
And fail while Freedom fails,
Enduring waste and lawlessness,
And the rule of the weak and the blind,
Dies in the hope of building earth,
Like the coral insect, for the temple
To stand on at the last.
And I swear that Freedom will wage to the end
The war for making every soul
Wise and strong and as fit to rule
As Plato's lofty guardians[†]
In a world republic girdled!

The Unknown

YE ASPIRING ONES, listen to the story of the unknown
Who lies here with no stone to mark the place.
As a boy reckless and wanton,
Wandering with gun in hand through the forest
Near the mansion of Aaron Hatfield,
I shot a hawk perched on the top
Of a dead tree.
He fell with guttural cry
At my feet, his wing broken.
Then I put him in a cage
Where he lived many days cawing angrily at me
When I offered him food.
Daily I search the realms of Hades†
For the soul of the hawk,
That I may offer him the friendship
Of one whom life wounded and caged.

Alexander Throckmorton

IN YOUTH MY wings were strong and tireless,
But I did not know the mountains.
In age I knew the mountains
But my weary wings could not follow my vision—
Genius is wisdom and youth.†

Jonathan Swift Somers[†]*

AFTER YOU HAVE enriched your soul
To the highest point,
With books, thought, suffering, the understanding of many personalities,
The power to interpret glances, silences,
The pauses in momentous transformations,
The genius of divination and prophecy;
So that you feel able at times to hold the world
In the hollow of your hand;
Then, if, by the crowding of so many powers
Into the compass of your soul,
Your soul takes fire,
And in the conflagration of your soul
The evil of the world is lighted up and made clear—
Be thankful if in that hour of supreme vision
Life does not fiddle.

*Author of THE SPOONIAD

Widow McFarlane

I WAS THE Widow McFarlane,
Weaver of carpets for all the village.
And I pity you still at the loom[†] of life,
You who are singing to the shuttle
And lovingly watching the work of your hands,
If you reach the day of hate, of terrible truth.
For the cloth of life is woven, you know,
To a pattern hidden under the loom—
A pattern you never see!
And you weave high-hearted, singing, singing,
You guard the threads of love and friendship
For noble figures in gold and purple.[†]
And long after other eyes can see
You have woven a moon-white strip of cloth,
You laugh in your strength, for Hope o'erlays it
With shapes of love and beauty.
The loom stops short! The pattern's out!
You're alone in the room! You have woven a shroud!
And hate of it lays you in it.

Carl Hamblin

THE PRESS OF the Spoon River *Clarion* was wrecked,
And I was tarred and feathered,
For publishing this on the day the Anarchists[†] were hanged in Chicago:
"I saw a beautiful woman with bandaged eyes
Standing on the steps of a marble temple.
Great multitudes passed in front of her,
Lifting their faces to her imploringly.
In her left hand she held a sword.
She was brandishing the sword,
Sometimes striking a child, again a laborer,
Again a slinking woman, again a lunatic.
In her right hand she held a scale;
Into the scale pieces of gold were tossed
By those who dodged the strokes of the sword.
A man in a black gown read from a manuscript:
"She is no respecter of persons."
Then a youth wearing a red cap
Leaped to her side and snatched away the bandage.
And lo, the lashes had been eaten away
From the oozy eye-lids;
The eye-balls were seared with a milky mucus;
The madness of a dying soul
Was written on her face—
But the multitude saw why she wore the bandage."[†]

Editor Whedon

TO BE ABLE to see every side of every question;
To be on every side, to be everything, to be nothing long;
To pervert truth, to ride it for a purpose,
To use great feelings and passions of the human family
For base designs, for cunning ends,
To wear a mask like the Greek actors—
Your eight-page paper—behind which you huddle,
Bawling through the megaphone of big type:
"This is I, the giant."
Thereby also living the life of a sneak-thief,
Poisoned with the anonymous words
Of your clandestine soul.
To scratch dirt over scandal for money,
And exhume it to the winds for revenge,
Or to sell papers,
Crushing reputations, or bodies, if need be,
To win at any cost, save your own life.
To glory in demoniac power, ditching civilization,
As a paranoiac boy puts a log on the track
And derails the express train.
To be an editor, as I was.
Then to lie here close by the river over the place
Where the sewage flows from the village,
And the empty cans and garbage are dumped,
And abortions are hidden.

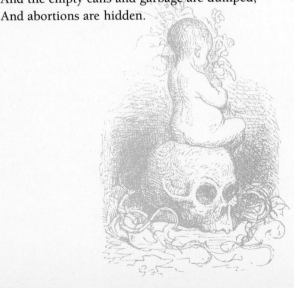

Eugene Carman

RHODES' SLAVE! SELLING shoes and gingham,
Flour and bacon, overalls, clothing, all day long
For fourteen hours a day for three hundred and thirteen days
For more than twenty years.
Saying "Yes'm" and "Yes, sir", and "Thank you"
A thousand times a day, and all for fifty dollars a month.
Living in this stinking room in the rattle-trap "Commercial."
And compelled to go to Sunday School, and to listen
To the Rev. Abner Peet one hundred and four times a year
For more than an hour at a time,
Because Thomas Rhodes ran the church
As well as the store and the bank.
So while I was tying my neck-tie that morning
I suddenly saw myself in the glass:
My hair all gray, my face like a sodden pie.
So I cursed and cursed: You damned old thing!
You cowardly dog! You rotten pauper!
You Rhodes' slave! Till Roger Baughman
Thought I was having a fight with some one,
And looked through the transom just in time
To see me fall on the floor in a heap
From a broken vein in my head.

Clarence Fawcett

THE SUDDEN DEATH of Eugene Carman
Put me in line to be promoted to fifty dollars a month,
And I told my wife and children that night.
But it didn't come, and so I thought
Old Rhodes suspected me of stealing
The blankets I took and sold on the side
For money to pay a doctor's bill for my little girl.
Then like a bolt old Rhodes accused me,
And promised me mercy for my family's sake
If I confessed, and so I confessed,
And begged him to keep it out of the papers,
And I asked the editors, too.
That night at home the constable took me
And every paper, except the *Clarion*,
Wrote me up as a thief
Because old Rhodes was an advertiser
And wanted to make an example of me.
Oh! well, you know how the children cried,
And how my wife pitied and hated me,
And how I came to lie here.

W. Lloyd Garrison† Standard

VEGETARIAN, NON-RESISTANT, free-thinker, in ethics a Christian;
Orator apt at the rhine-stone rhythm of Ingersoll;†
Carnivorous, avenger, believer and pagan;
Continent, promiscuous, changeable, treacherous, vain,
Proud, with the pride that makes struggle a thing for laughter;
With heart cored out by the worm of theatric despair;
Wearing the coat of indifference to hide the shame of defeat;
I, child of the abolitionist† idealism—
A sort of *Brand* in a birth of half-and-half.
What other thing could happen when I defended
The patriot scamps who burned the court house,
That Spoon River might have a new one,
Than plead them guilty? When Kinsey Keene drove through
The card-board mask of my life with a spear of light,
What could I do but slink away, like the beast of myself
Which I raised from a whelp, to a corner and growl
The pyramid of my life was nought but a dune,
Barren and formless, spoiled at last by the storm.

Professor Newcomer

EVERYONE LAUGHED AT Col. Prichard
For buying an engine so powerful
That it wrecked itself, and wrecked the grinder
He ran it with.
But here is a joke of cosmic size:
The urge of nature that made a man
Evolve from his brain a spiritual life—
Oh miracle of the world!—
The very same brain with which the ape and wolf
Get food and shelter and procreate themselves.
Nature has made man do this,
In a world where she gives him nothing to do
After all—(though the strength of his soul goes round
In a futile waste of power,
To gear itself to the mills of the gods)—
But get food and shelter and procreate himself!

Ralph Rhodes

ALL THEY SAID was true:
I wrecked my father's bank with my loans
To dabble in wheat; but this was true—
I was buying wheat for him as well,
Who couldn't margin the deal in his name
Because of his church relationship.
And while George Reece was serving his term
I chased the will-o'-the-wisp of women,[†]
And the mockery of wine in New York.
It's deathly to sicken of wine and women
When nothing else is left in life.
But suppose your head is gray, and bowed
On a table covered with acrid stubs
Of cigarettes and empty glasses,
And a knock is heard, and you know it's the knock
So long drowned out by popping corks
And the pea-cock screams of demireps—
And you look up, and there's your Theft,
Who waited until your head was gray,
And your heart skipped beats to say to you:
The game is ended. I've called for you.
Go out on Broadway and be run over,
They'll ship you back to Spoon River.

Mickey M'Grew

IT WAS JUST like everything else in life:
Something outside myself drew me down,
My own strength never failed me.
Why, there was the time I earned the money
With which to go away to school,
And my father suddenly needed help
And I had to give him all of it.
Just so it went till I ended up
A man-of-all-work in Spoon River.
Thus when I got the water-tower cleaned,
And they hauled me up the seventy feet,
I unhooked the rope from my waist,
And laughingly flung my giant arms
Over the smooth steel lips of the top of the tower—
But they slipped from the treacherous slime,
 And down, down, down, I plunged
Through bellowing darkness!

Rosie Roberts

I WAS SICK, but more than that, I was mad
At the crooked police, and the crooked game of life.
So I wrote to the Chief of Police at Peoria:
"I am here in my girlhood home in Spoon River,
Gradually wasting away.
But come and take me, I killed the son
Of the merchant prince, in Madam Lou's
And the papers that said he killed himself
In his home while cleaning a hunting gun—
Lied like the devil to hush up scandal,
For the bribe of advertising.
In my room I shot him, at Madam Lou's,
Because he knocked me down when I said
That, in spite of all the money he had,
I'd see my lover that night."

Oscar Hummel

I STAGGERED ON through darkness,
There was a hazy sky, a few stars
Which I followed as best I could.
It was nine o'clock, I was trying to get home.
But somehow I was lost,
Though really keeping the road.
Then I reeled through a gate and into a yard,
And called at the top of my voice:
"Oh, Fiddler! Oh, Mr. Jones!"
(I thought it was his house and he would show me the way home.)
But who should step out but A. D. Blood,
In his night shirt, waving a stick of wood,
And roaring about the cursed saloons,
And the criminals they made?
"You drunken Oscar Hummel," he said,
As I stood there weaving to and fro,
Taking the blows from the stick in his hand
Till I dropped down dead at his feet.

Roscoe Purkapile

SHE LOVED ME. Oh! how she loved me!
I never had a chance to escape
From the day she first saw me.
But then after we were married I thought
She might prove her mortality and let me out,
Or she might divorce me.
But few die, none resign.
Then I ran away and was gone a year on a lark.
But she never complained. She said all would be well,
That I would return. And I did return.
I told her that while taking a row in a boat
I had been captured near Van Buren Street
By pirates on Lake Michigan,
And kept in chains, so I could not write her.
She cried and kissed me, and said it was cruel,
Outrageous, inhuman!
I then concluded our marriage
Was a divine dispensation
And could not be dissolved,
Except by death.
I was right.†

Mrs. Purkapile

HE RAN AWAY and was gone for a year.
When he came home he told me the silly story
Of being kidnapped by pirates on Lake Michigan
And kept in chains so he could not write me.
I pretended to believe it, though I knew very well
What he was doing, and that he met
The milliner, Mrs. Williams, now and then
When she went to the city to buy goods, as she said.
But a promise is a promise
And marriage is marriage,
And out of respect for my own character
I refused to be drawn into a divorce
By the scheme of a husband who had merely grown tired
Of his marital vow and duty.

Josiah Tompkins

I WAS WELL known and much beloved
And rich, as fortunes are reckoned
In Spoon River, where I had lived and worked.
That was the home for me,
Though all my children had flown afar—
Which is the way of Nature—all but one.
The boy, who was the baby, stayed at home,
To be my help in my failing years
And the solace of his mother.
But I grew weaker, as he grew stronger,
And he quarreled with me about the business,
And his wife said I was a hindrance to it;
And he won his mother to see as he did,
Till they tore me up to be transplanted
With them to her girlhood home in Missouri.
And so much of my fortune was gone at last,
Though I made the will just as he drew it,
He profited little by it.

Mrs. Kessler

MR. KESSLER, YOU know, was in the army,
And he drew six dollars a month as a pension,
And stood on the corner talking politics,
Or sat at home reading Grant's Memoirs;[†]
And I supported the family by washing,
Learning the secrets of all the people
From their curtains, counterpanes, shirts and skirts.
For things that are new grow old at length,
They're replaced with better or none at all:
People are prospering or falling back.
And rents and patches widen with time;
No thread or needle can pace decay,
And there are stains that baffle soap,
And there are colors that run in spite of you,
Blamed though you are for spoiling a dress.
Handkerchiefs, napery, have their secrets—
The laundress, Life, knows all about it.
And l, who went to all the funerals
Held in Spoon River, swear I never
Saw a dead face without thinking it looked
Like something washed and ironed.[†]

Harmon Whitney

OUT OF THE lights and roar of cities,
Drifting down like a spark in Spoon River,
Burnt out with the fire of drink, and broken,
The paramour of a woman I took in self-contempt,
But to hide a wounded pride as well.
To be judged and loathed by a village of little minds—
I, gifted with tongues and wisdom,
Sunk here to the dust of the justice court,
A picker of rags in the rubbage of spites and wrongs,—
I, whom fortune smiled on! I in a village,
Spouting to gaping yokels pages of verse,
Out of the lore of golden years,
Or raising a laugh with a flash of filthy wit
When they bought the drinks to kindle my dying mind.
To be judged by you,
The soul of me hidden from you,
With its wound gangrened
By love for a wife who made the wound,
With her cold white bosom, treasonous, pure and hard,
Relentless to the last, when the touch of her hand,
At any time, might have cured me of the typhus,
Caught in the jungle of life where many are lost.
And only to think that my soul could not re-act,
Like Byron's did,† in song, in something noble,
But turned on itself like a tortured snake—
Judge me this way, O world!

Bert Kessler

I WINGED MY bird,
Though he flew toward the setting sun;
But just as the shot rang out, he soared
Up and up through the splinters of golden light,
Till he turned right over, feathers ruffled,
With some of the down of him floating near,
And fell like a plummet into the grass.
I tramped about, parting the tangles,
Till I saw a splash of blood on a stump,
And the quail lying close to the rotten roots.
I reached my hand, but saw no brier,
But something pricked and stung and numbed it.
And then, in a second, I spied the rattler—
The shutters wide in his yellow eyes,
The head of him arched, sunk back in the rings of him,
A circle of filth, the color of ashes,
Or oak leaves bleached under layers of leaves.
I stood like a stone as he shrank and uncoiled
And started to crawl beneath the stump,
When I fell limp in the grass.

Lambert Hutchins

I HAVE TWO monuments besides this granite obelisk:
One, the house I built on the hill,
With its spires, bay windows, and roof of slate;
The other, the lake-front in Chicago,
Where the railroad keeps a switching yard,
With whistling engines and crunching wheels,
And smoke and soot thrown over the city,
And the crash of cars along the boulevard,—
A blot like a hog-pen on the harbor
Of a great metropolis, foul as a sty.
I helped to give this heritage
To generations yet unborn, with my vote
In the House of Representatives,
And the lure of the thing was to be at rest
From the never-ending fright of need,
And to give my daughters gentle breeding,
And a sense of security in life.
But, you see, though I had the mansion house
And traveling passes and local distinction,
I could hear the whispers, whispers, whispers,
Wherever I went, and my daughters grew up
With a look as if some one were about to strike them;
And they married madly, helter-skelter,
Just to get out and have a change.
And what was the whole of the business worth?
Why, it wasn't worth a damn!

Lillian Stewart

I WAS THE daughter of Lambert Hutchins,
Born in a cottage near the grist-mill,
Reared in the mansion there on the hill,
With its spires, bay-windows, and roof of slate.
How proud my mother was of the mansion!
How proud of father's rise in the world!
And how my father loved and watched us,
And guarded our happiness.
But I believe the house was a curse,
For father's fortune was little beside it;
And when my husband found he had married
A girl who was really poor,
He taunted me with the spires,
And called the house a fraud on the world,
A treacherous lure to young men, raising hopes
Of a dowry not to be had;
And a man while selling his vote
Should get enough from the people's betrayal
To wall the whole of his family in.
He vexed my life till I went back home
And lived like an old maid till I died,
Keeping house for father.

Hortense Robbins

MY NAME USED to be in the papers daily
As having dined somewhere,
Or traveled somewhere,
Or rented a house in Paris,
Where I entertained the nobility.
I was forever eating or traveling,
Or taking the cure at Baden-Baden.†
Now I am here to do honor
To Spoon River, here beside the family whence I sprang.
No one cares now where I dined,
Or lived, or whom I entertained,
Or how often I took the cure at Baden-Baden.

Batterton Dobyns

DID MY WIDOW flit about
From Mackinac† to Los Angeles,
Resting and bathing and sitting an hour
Or more at the table over soup and meats
And delicate sweets and coffee?
I was cut down in my prime
From overwork and anxiety.
But I thought all along, whatever happens
I've kept my insurance up,
And there's something in the bank,
And a section of land in Manitoba.†
But just as I slipped I had a vision
In a last delirium:
I saw myself lying nailed in a box
With a white lawn tie and a boutonniere,
And my wife was sitting by a window
Some place afar overlooking the sea;
She seemed so rested, ruddy and fat,
Although her hair was white.
And she smiled and said to a colored waiter:
"Another slice of roast beef, George.
Here's a nickel for your trouble."

Jacob Godbey

How DID YOU feel, you libertarians,[†]
Who spent your talents rallying noble reasons
Around the saloon, as if Liberty
Was not to be found anywhere except at the bar
Or at a table, guzzling?
How did you feel, Ben Pantier, and the rest of you,
Who almost stoned me for a tyrant
Garbed as a moralist,
And as a wry-faced ascetic frowning upon Yorkshire pudding,
Roast beef and ale and good will and rosy cheer—
Things you never saw in a grog-shop in your life?
How did you feel after I was dead and gone,
And your goddess, Liberty, unmasked as a strumpet,
Selling out the streets of Spoon River
To the insolent giants
Who manned the saloons from afar?
Did it occur to you that personal liberty
Is liberty of the mind,
Rather than of the belly?

Walter Simmons

MY PARENTS THOUGHT that I would be
As great as Edison or greater:
For as a boy I made balloons
And wondrous kites and toys with clocks
And little engines with tracks to run on
And telephones of cans and thread.
I played the cornet and painted pictures,
Modeled in clay and took the part
Of the villain in the "Octoroon."†
But then at twenty-one I married
And had to live, and so, to live
I learned the trade of making watches
And kept the jewelry store on the square,
Thinking, thinking, thinking, thinking,—
Not of business, but of the engine
I studied the calculus to build.
And all Spoon River watched and waited
To see it work, but it never worked.
And a few kind souls believed my genius
Was somehow hampered by the store.
It wasn't true.
The truth was this:
I didn't have the brains.

Tom Beatty

I WAS A lawyer like Harmon Whitney
Or Kinsey Keene or Garrison Standard,
For I tried the rights of property,
Although by lamp-light, for thirty years,
In that poker room in the opera house.
And I say to you that Life's a gambler
Head and shoulders above us all.
No mayor alive can close the house.
And if you lose, you can squeal as you will;
You'll not get back your money.
He makes the percentage hard to conquer;
He stacks the cards to catch your weakness
And not to meet your strength.
And he gives you seventy years to play:
For if you cannot win in seventy
You cannot win at all.
So, if you lose, get out of the room—
Get out of the room when your time is up.
It's mean to sit and fumble the cards
And curse your losses, leaden-eyed,
Whining to try and try.

Roy Butler

IF THE LEARNED Supreme Court of Illinois
Got at the secret of every case
As well as it does a case of rape
It would be the greatest court in the world.
A jury, of neighbors mostly, with "Butch" Weldy
As foreman, found me guilty in ten minutes
And two ballots on a case like this:
Richard Bandle and I had trouble over a fence,
And my wife and Mrs. Bandle quarreled
As to whether Ipava[†] was a finer town than Table Grove.[†]
I awoke one morning with the love of God
Brimming over my heart, so I went to see Richard
To settle the fence in the spirit of Jesus Christ.
I knocked on the door, and his wife opened;
She smiled and asked me in; I entered—
She slammed the door and began to scream,
"Take your hands off, you low down varlet!"
Just then her husband entered.
I waved my hands, choked up with words.
He went for his gun, and I ran out.
But neither the Supreme Court nor my wife
Believed a word she said.

Searcy Foote

I WANTED TO go away to college
But rich Aunt Persis wouldn't help me.
So I made gardens and raked the lawns
And bought John Alden's books with my earnings
And toiled for the very means of life.
I wanted to marry Delia Prickett,
But how could I do it with what I earned?
And there was Aunt Persis more than seventy,
Who sat in a wheel-chair half alive,
With her throat so paralyzed, when she swallowed
The soup ran out of her mouth like a duck—
A gourmand yet, investing her income
In mortgages, fretting all the time
About her notes and rents and papers.
That day I was sawing wood for her,
And reading Proudhon[†] in between.
I went in the house for a drink of water,
And there she sat asleep in her chair,
And Proudhon lying on the table,
And a bottle of chloroform on the book,
She used sometimes for an aching tooth!
I poured the chloroform on a handkerchief
And held it to her nose till she died.[†]—
Oh Delia, Delia, you and Proudhon
Steadied my hand, and the coroner
Said she died of heart failure.
I married Delia and got the money—
A joke on you, Spoon River?

Edmund Pollard

I WOULD I had thrust my hands of flesh
Into the disk-flowers bee-infested,
Into the mirror-like core of fire
Of the light of life, the sun of delight.
For what are anthers worth or petals
Or halo-rays? Mockeries, shadows
Of the heart of the flower, the central flame!
All is yours, young passer-by;
Enter the banquet room with the thought;
Don't sidle in as if you were doubtful
Whether you're welcome—the feast is yours!
Nor take but a little, refusing more
With a bashful "Thank you," when you're hungry.
Is your soul alive? Then let it feed!
Leave no balconies where you can climb;
Nor milk-white bosoms where you can rest;
Nor golden heads with pillows to share;
Nor wine cups while the wine is sweet;
Nor ecstasies of body or soul,
You will die, no doubt, but die while living
In depths of azure, rapt and mated,
Kissing the queen-bee, Life!

Thomas Trevelyan

READING IN OVID[†] the sorrowful story of Itys,
Son of the love of Tereus and Procne, slain
For the guilty passion of Tereus for Philomela,
The flesh of him served to Tereus by Procne,
And the wrath of Tereus, the murderess pursuing
Till the gods made Philomela a nightingale,
Lute of the rising moon, and Procne a swallow[†]
Oh livers and artists of Hellas centuries gone,
Sealing in little thuribles dreams and wisdom,
Incense beyond all price, forever fragrant,
A breath whereof makes clear the eyes of the soul!
How I inhaled its sweetness here in Spoon River!
The thurible opening when I had lived and learned
How all of us kill the children of love, and all of us,
Knowing not what we do, devour their flesh;
And all of us change to singers, although it be
But once in our lives, or change—alas!—to swallows,
To twitter amid cold winds and falling leaves!

Percival Sharp

OBSERVE THE CLASPED hands!
Are they hands of farewell or greeting,
Hands that I helped or hands that helped me?
Would it not be well to carve a hand
With an inverted thumb, like Elagabalus?[†]
And yonder is a broken chain,
The weakest-link idea perhaps—but what was it?
And lambs, some lying down,
Others standing, as if listening to the shepherd—
Others bearing a cross, one foot lifted up—
Why not chisel a few shambles?
And fallen columns! Carve the pedestal, please,
Or the foundations; let us see the cause of the fall.
And compasses and mathematical instruments,
In irony of the under tenants' ignorance
Of determinants and the calculus of variations.
And anchors, for those who never sailed.
And gates ajar—yes, so they were;
You left them open and stray goats entered your garden.
And an eye watching like one of the Arimaspi[†]—
So did you—with one eye.
And angels blowing trumpets—you are heralded—
It is your horn and your angel and your family's estimate.
It is all very well, but for myself I know
I stirred certain vibrations in Spoon River
Which are my true epitaph, more lasting than stone.

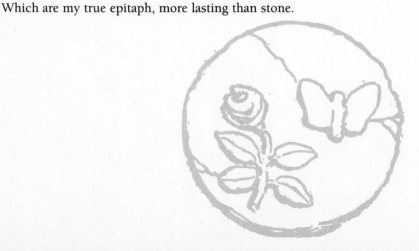

Hiram Scates

I TRIED TO win the nomination
For president of the County-board
And I made speeches all over the County
Denouncing Solomon Purple, my rival,
As an enemy of the people,
In league with the master-foes of man.
Young idealists, broken warriors,
Hobbling on one crutch of hope,
Souls that stake their all on the truth,
Losers of worlds at heaven's bidding,
Flocked about me and followed my voice
As the savior of the County.
But Solomon won the nomination;
And then I faced about,
And rallied my followers to his standard,
And made him victor, made him King
Of the Golden Mountain with the door
Which closed on my heels just as I entered,
Flattered by Solomon's invitation,
To be the County-board's secretary.
And out in the cold stood all my followers:
Young idealists, broken warriors
Hobbling on one crutch of hope—
Souls that staked their all on the truth,
Losers of worlds at heaven's bidding,
Watching the Devil kick the Millennium
Over the Golden Mountain.

Peleg Poague

HORSES AND MEN are just alike.
There was my stallion, Billy Lee,
Black as a cat and trim as a deer,
With an eye of fire, keen to start,
And he could hit the fastest speed
Of any racer around Spoon River.
But just as you'd think he couldn't lose,
With his lead of fifty yards or more,
He'd rear himself and throw the rider,
And fall back over, tangled up,
Completely gone to pieces.
You see he was a perfect fraud:
He couldn't win, he couldn't work,
He was too light to haul or plow with,
And no one wanted colts from him.
And when I tried to drive him—well,
He ran away and killed me.

Jeduthan Hawley

THERE WOULD BE a knock at the door
And I would arise at midnight and go to the shop,
Where belated travelers would hear me hammering
Sepulchral boards and tacking satin.
And often I wondered who would go with me
To the distant land, our names the theme
For talk, in the same week, for I've observed
Two always go together.
Chase Henry was paired with Edith Conant;
And Jonathan Somers with Willie Metcalf;
And Editor Hamblin with Francis Turner,
When he prayed to live longer than Editor Whedon;
And Thomas Rhodes with widow McFarlane;
And Emily Sparks with Barry Holden;
And Oscar Hummel with Davis Matlock;
And Editor Whedon with Fiddler Jones;
And Faith Matheny with Dorcas Gustine.
And l, the solemnest man in town,
Stepped off with Daisy Fraser.

Abel Melveny

I BOUGHT EVERY kind of machine that's known—
Grinders, shellers, planters, mowers,
Mills and rakes and ploughs and threshers—
And all of them stood in the rain and sun,
Getting rusted, warped and battered,
For I had no sheds to store them in,
And no use for most of them.
And toward the last, when I thought it over,
There by my window, growing clearer
About myself, as my pulse slowed down,
And looked at one of the mills I bought—
Which I didn't have the slightest need of,
As things turned out, and I never ran—
A fine machine, once brightly varnished,
And eager to do its work,
Now with its paint washed off—
I saw myself as a good machine
That Life had never used.

Oaks Tutt

MY MOTHER WAS for woman's rights
And my father was the rich miller at London Mills.
I dreamed of the wrongs of the world and wanted to right them.
When my father died, I set out to see peoples and countries
In order to learn how to reform the world.
I traveled through many lands.
I saw the ruins of Rome,
And the ruins of Athens,
And the ruins of Thebes.
And I sat by moonlight amid the necropolis of Memphis.
There I was caught up by wings of flame,
And a voice from heaven said to me:
"Injustice, Untruth destroyed them. Go forth!
Preach Justice! Preach Truth!"
And I hastened back to Spoon River
To say farewell to my mother before beginning my work.
They all saw a strange light in my eye.
And by and by, when I talked, they discovered
What had come in my mind.
Then Jonathan Swift Somers challenged me to debate
The subject, (I taking the negative):
"Pontius Pilate,[†] the Greatest Philosopher of the World."
And he won the debate by saying at last,
"Before you reform the world, Mr. Tutt
Please answer the question of Pontius Pilate:
"What is Truth?"[†]

Elliott Hawkins

I LOOKED LIKE Abraham Lincoln.
I was one of you, Spoon River, in all fellowship,
But standing for the rights of property and for order.
A regular church attendant,
Sometimes appearing in your town meetings to warn you
Against the evils of discontent and envy,
And to denounce those who tried to destroy the Union,
And to point to the peril of the Knights of Labor.
My success and my example are inevitable influences
In your young men and in generations to come,
In spite of attacks of newspapers like the *Clarion*;
A regular visitor at Springfield,
When the Legislature was in session,
To prevent raids upon the railroads,
And the men building up the state.
Trusted by them and by you, Spoon River, equally
In spite of the whispers that I was a lobbyist.
Moving quietly through the world, rich and courted.
Dying at last, of course, but lying here
Under a stone with an open book carved upon it
And the words "*Of such is the Kingdom of Heaven.*"
And now, you world-savers, who reaped nothing in life
And in death have neither stones nor epitaphs,
How do you like your silence from mouths stopped
With the dust of my triumphant career?

Voltaire Johnson

WHY DID YOU bruise me with your rough places
If you did not want me to tell you about them?
And stifle me with your stupidities,
If you did not want me to expose them?
And nail me with the nails of cruelty,
If you did not want me to pluck the nails forth
And fling them in your faces?
And starve me because I refused to obey you,
If you did not want me to undermine your tyranny?
I might have been as soul serene
As William Wordsworth[†] except for you!
But what a coward you are, Spoon River,
When you drove me to stand in a magic circle
By the sword of Truth described!
And then to whine and curse your burns,
And curse my power who stood and laughed
Amid ironical lightening!

English Thornton

HERE! YOU SONS of the men
Who fought with Washington at Valley Forge,[†]
And whipped Black Hawk[†] at Starved Rock,[†]
Arise! Do battle with the descendants of those
Who bought land in the loop when it was waste sand,
And sold blankets and guns to the army of Grant,
And sat in legislatures in the early days,
Taking bribes from the railroads!
Arise! Do battle with the fops and bluffs,
The pretenders and figurantes of the society column
And the yokel souls whose daughters marry counts;
And the parasites on great ideas,
And the noisy riders of great causes,
And the heirs of ancient thefts.
Arise! And make the city yours,
And the State yours—
By God! If you do not destroy the vermin
My avenging ghost will wipe out
Your city and your state.

Enoch Dunlap

HOW MANY TIMES, during the twenty years
I was your leader, friends of Spoon River,
Did you neglect the convention and caucus,
And leave the burden on my hands
Of guarding and saving the people's cause?—
Sometimes because you were ill;
Or your grandmother was ill;
Or you drank too much and fell asleep;
Or else you said: "He is our leader,
All will be well; he fights for us;
We have nothing to do but follow."
But oh, how you cursed me when I fell,
And cursed me, saying I had betrayed you,
In leaving the caucus room for a moment,
When the people's enemies, there assembled,
Waited and watched for a chance to destroy
The Sacred Rights of the People.
You common rabble! I left the caucus
To go to the urinal!

Ida Frickey

NOTHING IN LIFE is alien to you:
I was a penniless girl from Summum
Who stepped from the morning train in Spoon River.
All the houses stood before me with closed doors
And drawn shades—l was barred out;
I had no place or part in any of them.
And I walked past the old McNeely mansion,
A castle of stone 'mid walks and gardens
With workmen about the place on guard
And the County and State upholding it
For its lordly owner, full of pride.
I was so hungry I had a vision:
I saw a giant pair of scissors
Dip from the sky, like the beam of a dredge,
And cut the house in two like a curtain.
But at the "Commercial" I saw a man,
Who winked at me as I asked for work—
It was Wash McNeely's son.
He proved the link in the chain of title
To half my ownership of the mansion,
Through a breach of promise suit—the scissors.
So, you see, the house, from the day I was born,
Was only waiting for me.

Seth Compton

WHEN I DIED, the circulating library
Which I built up for Spoon River,
And managed for the good of inquiring minds,
Was sold at auction on the public square,
As if to destroy the last vestige
Of my memory and influence.
For those of you who could not see the virtue
Of knowing Volney's "Ruins"[†] as well as Butler's "Analogy"[†]
And "Faust"[†] as well as "Evangeline,"[†]
Were really the power in the village,
And often you asked me
"What is the use of knowing the evil in the world?"
I am out of your way now, Spoon River,
Choose your own good and call it good.
For I could never make you see
That no one knows what is good
Who knows not what is evil;
And no one knows what is true
Who knows not what is false.[†]

Felix Schmidt

IT WAS ONLY a little house of two rooms—
Almost like a child's play-house—
With scarce five acres of ground around it;
And I had so many children to feed
And school and clothe, and a wife who was sick
From bearing children.
One day lawyer Whitney came along
And proved to me that Christian Dallman,
Who owned three thousand acres of land,
Had bought the eighty that adjoined me
In eighteen hundred and seventy-one
For eleven dollars, at a sale for taxes,
While my father lay in his mortal illness.
So the quarrel arose and I went to law.
But when we came to the proof,
A survey of the land showed clear as day
That Dallman's tax deed covered my ground
And my little house of two rooms.
It served me right for stirring him up.
I lost my case and lost my place.
I left the court room and went to work
As Christian Dallman's tenant.

Schrœder The Fisherman

I SAT ON the bank above Bernadotte[†]
And dropped crumbs in the water,
Just to see the minnows bump each other,
Until the strongest got the prize.
Or I went to my little pasture,
Where the peaceful swine were asleep in the wallow,
Or nosing each other lovingly,
And emptied a basket of yellow corn,
And watched them push and squeal and bite,
And trample each other to get the corn.
And I saw how Christian Dallman's farm,
Of more than three thousand acres,
Swallowed the patch of Felix Schmidt,
As a bass will swallow a minnow
And I say if there's anything in man—
Spirit, or conscience, or breath of God
That makes him different from fishes or hogs,
I'd like to see it work!

Richard Bone

WHEN I FIRST came to Spoon River
I did not know whether what they told me
Was true or false.
They would bring me the epitaph
And stand around the shop while I worked
And say "He was so kind," "He was so wonderful,"
"She was the sweetest woman," "He was a consistent Christian."
And I chiseled for them whatever they wished,
All in ignorance of the truth.
But later, as I lived among the people here,
I knew how near to the life
Were the epitaphs that were ordered for them as they died.
But still I chiseled whatever they paid me to chisel
And made myself party to the false chronicles
Of the stones,
Even as the historian does who writes
Without knowing the truth,
Or because he is influenced to hide it.[†]

Silas Dement

IT WAS MOON-LIGHT, and the earth sparkled
With new-fallen frost.
It was midnight and not a soul abroad.
Out of the chimney of the court-house
A grey-hound of smoke leapt and chased
The northwest wind.
I carried a ladder to the landing of the stairs
And leaned it against the frame of the trap-door
In the ceiling of the portico,
And I crawled under the roof and amid the rafters
And flung among the seasoned timbers
A lighted handful of oil-soaked waste.
Then I came down and slunk away.
In a little while the fire-bell rang—
Clang! Clang! Clang!
And the Spoon River ladder company
Came with a dozen buckets and began to pour water
On the glorious bon-fire, growing hotter
Higher and brighter, till the walls fell in,
And the limestone columns where Lincoln stood
Crashed like trees when the woodman fells them...
When I came back from Joliet[†]
There was a new court house with a dome.
For I was punished like all who destroy
The past for the sake of the future.

Dillard Sissman

THE BUZZARDS WHEEL slowly
In wide circles, in a sky
Faintly hazed as from dust from the road.
And a wind sweeps through the pasture where I lie
Beating the grass into long waves.
My kite is above the wind,
Though now and then it wobbles,
Like a man shaking his shoulders;
And the tail streams out momentarily,
Then sinks to rest.
And the buzzards wheel and wheel,
Sweeping the zenith with wide circles
Above my kite. And the hills sleep.
And a farm house, white as snow,
Peeps from green trees—far away.
And I watch my kite,
For the thin moon will kindle herself ere long,
Then she will swing like a pendulum dial
To the tail of my kite.
A spurt of flame like a water-dragon
Dazzles my eyes—
I am shaken as a banner!

Jonathan Houghton

THERE IS THE caw of a crow,
And the hesitant song of a thrush.
There is the tinkle of a cowbell far away,
And the voice of a plowman on Shipley's hill.
The forest beyond the orchard is still
With midsummer stillness;
And along the road a wagon chuckles,
Loaded with corn, going to Atterbury.†
And an old man sits under a tree asleep,
And an old woman crosses the road,
Coming from the orchard with a bucket of blackberries.
And a boy lies in the grass
Near the feet of the old man,
And looks up at the sailing clouds,
And longs, and longs, and longs
For what, he knows not:
For manhood, for life, for the unknown world!
Then thirty years passed,
And the boy returned worn out by life
And found the orchard vanished,
And the forest gone,
And the house made over,
And the roadway filled with dust from automobiles—
And himself desiring The Hill!

E. C. Culbertson

IS IT TRUE, Spoon River,
That in the hall-way of the New Court House
There is a tablet of bronze
Containing the embossed faces
Of Editor Whedon and Thomas Rhodes?
And is it true that my successful labors
In the County Board, without which
Not one stone would have been placed on another,
And the contributions out of my own pocket
To build the temple, are but memories among the people,
Gradually fading away, and soon to descend
With them to this oblivion where I lie?
In truth, I can so believe.
For it is a law of the Kingdom of Heaven
That whoso enters the vineyard at the eleventh hour
Shall receive a full day's pay.
And it is a law of the Kingdom of this World
That those who first oppose a good work
Seize it and make it their own,
When the corner-stone is laid,
And memorial tablets are erected.

Shack Dye

THE WHITE MEN played all sorts of jokes on me.
They took big fish off my hook
And put little ones on, while I was away
Getting a stringer, and made me believe
I hadn't seen aright the fish I had caught.
When Burr Robbins, circus came to town
They got the ring master to let a tame leopard
Into the ring, and made me believe
I was whipping a wild beast like Samson
When l, for an offer of fifty dollars,
Dragged him out to his cage.
One time I entered my blacksmith shop
And shook as I saw some horse-shoes crawling
Across the floor, as if alive—
Walter Simmons had put a magnet
Under the barrel of water.
Yet everyone of you, you white men,
Was fooled about fish and about leopards too,
And you didn't know any more than the horse-shoes did
What moved you about Spoon River.†

Hildrup Tubbs

I MADE TWO fights for the people.
First I left my party, bearing the gonfalon
Of independence, for reform, and was defeated.
Next I used my rebel strength
To capture the standard of my old party—
And I captured it, but I was defeated.
Discredited and discarded, misanthropical,
I turned to the solace of gold
And I used my remnant of power
To fasten myself like a saprophyte
Upon the putrescent carcass
Of Thomas Rhodes' bankrupt bank,
As assignee of the fund.
Everyone now turned from me.
My hair grew white,
My purple lusts grew gray,
Tobacco and whisky lost their savor
And for years Death ignored me
As he does a hog.

Henry Tripp

THE BANK BROKE and I lost my savings.
I was sick of the tiresome game in Spoon River
And I made up my mind to run away
And leave my place in life and my family;
But just as the midnight train pulled in,
Quick off the steps jumped Cully Green
And Martin Vise, and began to fight
To settle their ancient rivalry,
Striking each other with fists that sounded
Like the blows of knotted clubs.
Now it seemed to me that Cully was winning,
When his bloody face broke into a grin
Of sickly cowardice, leaning on Martin
And whining out "We're good friends, Mart,
You know that I'm your friend."
But a terrible punch from Martin knocked him
Around and around and into a heap.
And then they arrested me as a witness,
And I lost my train and staid in Spoon River
To wage my battle of life to the end.
Oh, Cully Green, you were my savior—
You, so ashamed and drooped for years,
Loitering listless about the streets,
And tying rags 'round your festering soul,
Who failed to fight it out.

Granville Calhoun

I WANTED TO be County Judge
One more term, so as to round out a service
Of thirty years.
But my friends left me and joined my enemies,
And they elected a new man.
Then a spirit of revenge seized me,
And I infected my four sons with it,
And I brooded upon retaliation,
Until the great physician, Nature,
Smote me through with paralysis
To give my soul and body a rest.
Did my sons get power and money?
Did they serve the people or yoke them,
To till and harvest fields of self?
For how could they ever forget
My face at my bed-room window,
Sitting helpless amid my golden cages
Of singing canaries,
Looking at the old court-house?

Henry C. Calhoun

I REACHED THE highest place in Spoon River,
But through what bitterness of spirit!
The face of my father, sitting speechless,
Child-like, watching his canaries,
And looking at the court-house window
Of the county judge's room,
And his admonitions to me to seek
My own in life, and punish Spoon River
To avenge the wrong the people did him,
Filled me with furious energy
To seek for wealth and seek for power.
But what did he do but send me along
The path that leads to the grove of the Furies?[†]
I followed the path and I tell you this:
On the way to the grove you'll pass the Fates,[†]
Shadow-eyed, bent over their weaving.
Stop for a moment, and if you see
The thread of revenge leap out of the shuttle,
Then quickly snatch from Atropos[†]
The shears and cut it, lest your sons,
And the children of them and their children
Wear the envenomed robe.

Alfred Moir

WHY WAS I not devoured by self-contempt,
And rotted down by indifference
And impotent revolt like Indignation Jones?
Why, with all of my errant steps,
Did I miss the fate of Willard Fluke?
And why, though I stood at Burchard's bar,
As a sort of decoy for the house to the boys
To buy the drinks, did the curse of drink
Fall on me like rain that runs off,
Leaving the soul of me dry and clean?
And why did I never kill a man
Like Jack McGuire?
But instead I mounted a little in life,
And I owe it all to a book I read.
But why did I go to Mason City,[†]
Where I chanced to see the book in a window,
With its garish cover luring my eye?
And why did my soul respond to the book,
As I read it over and over?[†]

Perry Zoll

MY THANKS, FRIENDS of the County Scientific Association,
For this modest boulder,
And its little tablet of bronze.
Twice I tried to join your honored body,
And was rejected
And when my little brochure
On the intelligence of plants
Began to attract attention
You almost voted me in.
After that I grew beyond the need of you
And your recognition.
Yet I do not reject your memorial stone,
Seeing that I should, in so doing,
Deprive you of honor to yourselves.

Dippold the Optician

WHAT DO YOU see now?
Globes of red, yellow, purple.
Just a moment! And now?
My father and mother and sisters.
Yes! And now?
Knights at arms, beautiful women, kind faces.
Try this.
A field of grain—a city.
Very good! And now?
A young woman with angels bending over her.
A heavier lens! And now?
Many women with bright eyes and open lips.
Try this.
Just a goblet on a table.
Oh I see! Try this lens!
Just an open space—I see nothing in particular.
Well, now!
Pine trees, a lake, a summer sky.
That's better. And now?
A book.
Read a page for me.
I can't. My eyes are carried beyond the page.
Try this lens.
Depths of air.
Excellent! And now!
Light, just light making everything below it a toy world.
Very well, we'll make the glasses accordingly.

Magrady Graham

TELL ME, WAS Altgeld[†] elected Governor?
For when the returns began to come in
And Cleveland was sweeping the East,
It was too much for you, poor old heart,
Who had striven for democracy
In the long, long years of defeat.
And like a watch that is worn
I felt you growing slower until you stopped.
Tell me, was Altgeld elected,
And what did he do?
Did they bring his head on a platter to a dancer,[†]
Or did he triumph for the people?
For when I saw him
And took his hand,
The child-like blueness of his eyes
Moved me to tears,
And there was an air of eternity about him,
Like the cold, clear light that rests at dawn
On the hills!

Archibald Higbie

I LOATHED YOU, Spoon River. I tried to rise above you,
I was ashamed of you. I despised you
As the place of my nativity.
And there in Rome, among the artists,
Speaking Italian, speaking French,
I seemed to myself at times to be free
Of every trace of my origin.
I seemed to be reaching the heights of art
And to breathe the air that the masters breathed,
And to see the world with their eyes.
But still they'd pass my work and say:
"What are you driving at, my friend?
Sometimes the face looks like Apollo's,†
At others it has a trace of Lincoln's."†
There was no culture, you know, in Spoon River
And I burned with shame and held my peace.
And what could I do, all covered over
And weighted down with western soil,
Except aspire, and pray for another
Birth in the world, with all of Spoon River
Rooted out of my soul?

Tom Merritt

AT FIRST I suspected something—
She acted so calm and absent-minded.
And one day I heard the back door shut
As I entered the front, and I saw him slink
Back of the smokehouse into the lot,
And run across the field.
And I meant to kill him on sight.
But that day, walking near Fourth Bridge
Without a stick or a stone at hand,
All of a sudden I saw him standing
Scared to death, holding his rabbits,
And all I could say was, "Don't, Don't, Don't,"
As he aimed and fired at my heart.

Mrs. Merritt

SILENT BEFORE THE jury,
Returning no word to the judge when he asked me
If I had aught to say against the sentence,
Only shaking my head.
What could I say to people who thought
That a woman of thirty-five was at fault
When her lover of nineteen killed her husband?
Even though she had said to him over and over,
"Go away, Elmer, go far away,
I have maddened your brain with the gift of my body:
You will do some terrible thing."
And just as I feared, he killed my husband;
With which I had nothing to do, before God!
Silent for thirty years in prison!
And the iron gates of Joliet†
Swung as the gray and silent trusties
Carried me out in a coffin.

Elmer Karr

WHAT BUT THE love of God could have softened
And made forgiving the people of Spoon River
Toward me who wronged the bed of Thomas Merritt
And murdered him beside?
Oh, loving hearts that took me in again
When I returned from fourteen years in prison!
Oh, helping hands that in the church received me,
And heard with tears my penitent confession,
Who took the sacrament of bread and wine!
Repent, ye living ones, and rest with Jesus.†

Elizabeth Childers

DUST OF MY dust,
And dust with my dust,
O, child who died as you entered the world,
Dead with my death!
Not knowing Breath, though you tried so hard,
With a heart that beat when you lived with me,
And stopped when you left me for Life.
It is well, my child. For you never traveled
The long, long way that begins with school days,
When little fingers blur under the tears
That fall on the crooked letters.
And the earliest wound, when a little mate
Leaves you alone for another;
And sickness, and the face of Fear by the bed;
The death of a father or mother;
Or shame for them, or poverty;
The maiden sorrow of school days ended;
And eyeless Nature that makes you drink
From the cup of Love, though you know it's poisoned;
To whom would your flower-face have been lifted?
Botanist, weakling? Cry of what blood to yours?—
Pure or foul, for it makes no matter,
It's blood that calls to our blood.
And then your children—oh, what might they be?
And what your sorrow? Child! Child!
Death is better than Life.

Edith Conant

WE STAND ABOUT this place—we, the memories;
And shade our eyes because we dread to read:
"June 17th, 1884, aged 21 years and 3 days."
And all things are changed.
And we—we, the memories, stand here for ourselves alone,
For no eye marks us, or would know why we are here.
Your husband is dead, your sister lives far away,
Your father is bent with age;
He has forgotten you, he scarcely leaves the house
Any more.
No one remembers your exquisite face,
Your lyric voice!
How you sang, even on the morning you were stricken,
With piercing sweetness, with thrilling sorrow,
Before the advent of the child which died with you.
It is all forgotten, save by us, the memories,
Who are forgotten by the world.
All is changed, save the river and the hill—
Even they are changed.
Only the burning sun and the quiet stars are the same.
And we—we, the memories, stand here in awe,
Our eyes closed with the weariness of tears—
In immeasurable weariness!

Charles Webster

THE PINE WOODS on the hill,
And the farmhouse miles away,
Showed clear as though behind a lens
Under a sky of peacock blue!
But a blanket of cloud by afternoon
Muffled the earth. And you walked the road
And the clover field, where the only sound
Was the cricket's liquid tremolo.
Then the sun went down between great drifts
Of distant storms. For a rising wind
Swept clean the sky and blew the flames
Of the unprotected stars;
And swayed the russet moon,
Hanging between the rim of the hill
And the twinkling boughs of the apple orchard.
You walked the shore in the thought
Where the throats of the waves were like whip-poor-wills
Singing beneath the water and crying
To the wash of the wind in the cedar trees,
Till you stood, too full for tears, by the cot,
And looking up saw Jupiter,
Tipping the spire of the giant pine,
And looking down saw my vacant chair,
Rocked by the wind on the lonely porch—
Be brave, Beloved!

Father Malloy

YOU ARE OVER there, Father Malloy,
Where holy ground is, and the cross marks every grave,
Not here with us on the hill—
Us of wavering faith, and clouded vision
And drifting hope, and unforgiven sins.
You were so human, Father Malloy,
Taking a friendly glass sometimes with us,
Siding with us who would rescue Spoon River
From the coldness and the dreariness of village morality.
You were like a traveler who brings a little box of sand
From the wastes about the pyramids
And makes them real and Egypt real.
You were a part of and related to a great past,
And yet you were so close to many of us.
You believed in the joy of life.
You did not seem to be ashamed of the flesh.
You faced life as it is,
And as it changes.
Some of us almost came to you, Father Malloy,
Seeing how your church had divined the heart,
And provided for it,
Through Peter the Flame,
Peter the Rock.†

Ami Green

NOT "A YOUTH with hoary head and haggard eye,"
But an old man with a smooth skin
And black hair!
I had the face of a boy as long as I lived,
And for years a soul that was stiff and bent,
In a world which saw me just as a jest,
To be hailed familiarly when it chose,
And loaded up as a man when it chose,
Being neither man nor boy.
In truth it was soul as well as body
Which never matured, and I say to you
That the much-sought prize of eternal youth
Is just arrested growth.

Calvin Campbell

YE WHO ARE kicking against Fate,
Tell me how it is that on this hill-side,
Running down to the river,
Which fronts the sun and the south-wind,
This plant draws from the air and soil
Poison and becomes poison ivy?
And this plant draws from the same air and soil
Sweet elixirs and colors and becomes arbutus?
And both flourish?
You may blame Spoon River for what it is,
But whom do you blame for the will in you
That feeds itself and makes you dock-weed,
Jimpson, dandelion or mullen
And which can never use any soil or air
So as to make you jessamine or wistaria?

Henry Layton

WHOEVER THOU ART who passest by
Know that my father was gentle,
And my mother was violent,
While I was born the whole of such hostile halves,
Not intermixed and fused,
But each distinct, feebly soldered together.
Some of you saw me as gentle,
Some as violent,
Some as both.
But neither half of me wrought my ruin.
It was the falling asunder of halves,
Never a part of each other,
That left me a lifeless soul.

Harlan Sewall

YOU NEVER UNDERSTOOD, O unknown one,
Why it was I repaid
Your devoted friendship and delicate ministrations
First with diminished thanks,
Afterward by gradually withdrawing my presence from you,
So that I might not be compelled to thank you,
And then with silence which followed upon
Our final Separation.
You had cured my diseased soul. But to cure it
You saw my disease, you knew my secret,
And that is why I fled from you.
For though when our bodies rise from pain
We kiss forever the watchful hands
That gave us wormwood, while we shudder
For thinking of the wormwood,
A soul that's cured is a different matter,
For there we'd blot from memory
The soft-toned words, the searching eyes,
And stand forever oblivious,
Not so much of the sorrow itself
As of the hand that healed it.

Ippolit Konovaloff

I WAS A gun-smith in Odessa.[†]
One night the police broke in the room
Where a group of us were reading Spencer.[†]
And seized our books and arrested us.
But I escaped and came to New York
And thence to Chicago, and then to Spoon River,
Where I could study my Kant[†] in peace
And eke out a living repairing guns!
Look at my moulds! My architectonics!
One for a barrel, one for a hammer,
And others for other parts of a gun!
Well, now suppose no gun-smith living
Had anything else but duplicate moulds
Of these I show you—well, all guns
Would be just alike, with a hammer to hit
The cap and a barrel to carry the shot,
All acting alike for themselves, and all
Acting against each other alike.
And there would be your world of guns!
Which nothing could ever free from itself
Except a Moulder with different moulds
To mould the metal over.

Henry Phipps

I WAS THE Sunday-school superintendent,
The dummy president of the wagon works
And the canning factory,
Acting for Thomas Rhodes and the banking clique;
My son the cashier of the bank,
Wedded to Rhodes' daughter,
My week days spent in making money,
My Sundays at church and in prayer.
In everything a cog in the wheel of things-as-they-are:
Of money, master and man, made white
With the paint of the Christian creed.
And then:
The bank collapsed. I stood and hooked at the wrecked machine—
The wheels with blow-holes stopped with putty and painted;
The rotten bolts, the broken rods;
And only the hopper for souls fit to be used again
In a new devourer of life, when newspapers, judges and money-magicians
Build over again.
I was stripped to the bone, but I lay in the Rock of Ages,
Seeing now through the game, no longer a dupe,
And knowing "'the upright shall dwell in the land
But the years of the wicked shall be shortened."
Then suddenly, Dr. Meyers discovered
A cancer in my liver.
I was not, after all, the particular care of God!
Why, even thus standing on a peak
Above the mists through which I had climbed,
And ready for larger life in the world,
Eternal forces
Moved me on with a push.

Harry Wilmans

I WAS JUST turned twenty-one,
And Henry Phipps, the Sunday-school superintendent,
Made a speech in Bindle's Opera House.
"The honor of the flag must be upheld," he said,
"Whether it be assailed by a barbarous tribe of Tagalogs†
Or the greatest power in Europe."
And we cheered and cheered the speech and the flag he waved
As he spoke.
And I went to the war in spite of my father,
And followed the flag till I saw it raised
By our camp in a rice field near Manila,†
And all of us cheered and cheered it.
But there were flies and poisonous things;
And there was the deadly water,
And the cruel heat,
And the sickening, putrid food;
And the smell of the trench just back of the tents
Where the soldiers went to empty themselves;
And there were the whores who followed us, full of syphilis;
And beastly acts between ourselves or alone,
With bullying, hatred, degradation among us,
And days of loathing and nights of fear
To the hour of the charge through the steaming swamp,
Following the flag,
Till I fell with a scream, shot through the guts.
Now there's a flag over me in Spoon River!
A flag! A flag!

John Wasson

OH! THE DEW-WET grass of the meadow in North Carolina
Through which Rebecca followed me wailing, wailing,
One child in her arms, and three that ran along wailing,
Lengthening out the farewell to me off to the war with the British,
And then the long, hard years down to the day of Yorktown.
And then my search for Rebecca,
Finding her at last in Virginia,
Two children dead in the meanwhile.
We went by oxen to Tennessee,
Thence after years to Illinois,
At last to Spoon River.
We cut the buffalo grass,
We felled the forests,
We built the school houses, built the bridges,
Leveled the roads and tilled the fields
Alone with poverty, scourges, death—
If Harry Wilmans who fought the Filipinos
Is to have a flag on his grave
Take it from mine!†

Many Soldiers

THE IDEA DANCED before us as a flag;
The sound of martial music;
The thrill of carrying a gun;
Advancement in the world on coming home;
A glint of glory, wrath for foes;
A dream of duty to country or to God.
But these were things in ourselves, shining before us,
They were not the power behind us,
Which was the Almighty hand of Life,
Like fire at earth's center making mountains,
Or pent up waters that cut them through.
Do you remember the iron band
The blacksmith, Shack Dye, welded
Around the oak on Bennet's lawn,
From which to swing a hammock,
That daughter Janet might repose in, reading
On summer afternoons?
And that the growing tree at last
Sundered the iron band?
But not a cell in all the tree
Knew aught save that it thrilled with life,
Nor cared because the hammock fell
In the dust with Milton's† Poems.†

Godwin James

HARRY WILMANS! YOU who fell in a swamp
Near Manila, following the flag
You were not wounded by the greatness of a dream,
Or destroyed by ineffectual work,
Or driven to madness by Satanic snags;
You were not torn by aching nerves,
Nor did you carry great wounds to your old age.
You did not starve, for the government fed you.
You did not suffer yet cry "forward"
To an army which you led
Against a foe with mocking smiles,
Sharper than bayonets. You were not smitten down
By invisible bombs. You were not rejected
By those for whom you were defeated.
You did not eat the savorless bread
Which a poor alchemy had made from ideals.
You went to Manila, Harry Wilmans,
While I enlisted in the bedraggled army
Of bright-eyed, divine youths,
Who surged forward, who were driven back and fell
Sick, broken, crying, shorn of faith,
Following the flag of the Kingdom of Heaven.
You and I, Harry Wilmans, have fallen
In our several ways, not knowing
Good from bad, defeat from victory,
Nor what face it is that smiles
Behind the demoniac mask.

Lyman King

YOU MAY THINK, passer-by, that Fate
Is a pit-fall outside of yourself,
Around which you may walk by the use of foresight
And wisdom.
Thus you believe, viewing the lives of other men,
As one who in God-like fashion bends over an anthill,
Seeing how their difficulties could be avoided.
But pass on into life:
In time you shall see Fate approach you
In the shape of your own image in the mirror;
Or you shall sit alone by your own hearth,
And suddenly the chair by you shall hold a guest,
And you shall know that guest
And read the authentic message of his eyes.

Caroline Branson

WITH OUR HEARTS like drifting suns, had we but walked,
As often before, the April fields till star-light
Silkened over with viewless gauze the darkness
Under the cliff, our trysting place in the wood,
Where the brook turns! Had we but passed from wooing
Like notes of music that run together, into winning,
In the inspired improvisation of love!
But to put back of us as a canticle ended
The rapt enchantment of the flesh,
In which our souls swooned, down, down,
Where time was not, nor space, nor ourselves—
Annihilated in love!
To leave these behind for a room with lamps:
And to stand with our Secret mocking itself,
And hiding itself amid flowers and mandolins,
Stared at by all between salad and coffee.
And to see him tremble, and feel myself
Prescient, as one who signs a bond—
Not flaming with gifts and pledges heaped
With rosy hands over his brow.
And then, O night! deliberate! unlovely!
With all of our wooing blotted out by the winning,
In a chosen room in an hour that was known to all!
Next day he sat so listless, almost cold,
So strangely changed, wondering why I wept,
Till a kind of sick despair and voluptuous madness
Seized us to make the pact of death.

A stalk of the earth-sphere,
Frail as star-light;
Waiting to be drawn once again
Into creation's stream.
But next time to be given birth
Gazed at by Raphael† and St. Francis†
Sometimes as they pass.
For I am their little brother,
To be known clearly face to face
Through a cycle of birth hereafter run.
You may know the seed and the soil;

You may feel the cold rain fall,
But only the earth-sphere, only heaven
Knows the secret of the seed
In the nuptial chamber under the soil.
Throw me into the stream again,
Give me another trial—
Save me, Shelley!

Anne Rutledge

OUT OF ME unworthy and unknown
The vibrations of deathless music;
"With malice toward none, with charity for all."[†]
Out of me the forgiveness of millions toward millions,
And the beneficent face of a nation
Shining with justice and truth.
I am Anne Rutledge[†] who sleep beneath these weeds,
Beloved in life of Abraham Lincoln,
Wedded to him, not through union,
But through separation.
Bloom forever, O Republic,
From the dust of my bosom!

Hamlet Micure

In a lingering fever many visions come to you:
I was in the little house again
With its great yard of clover
Running down to the board-fence,
Shadowed by the oak tree,
Where we children had our swing.
Yet the little house was a manor hall
Set in a lawn, and by the lawn was the sea.
I was in the room where little Paul
Strangled from diphtheria,
But yet it was not this room—
It was a sunny verandah enclosed
With mullioned windows
And in a chair sat a man in a dark cloak
With a face like Euripides.[†]
He had come to visit me, or I had gone to visit him—
I could not tell.
We could hear the beat of the sea, the clover nodded
Under a summer wind, and little Paul came
With clover blossoms to the window and smiled.
Then I said: "What is divine despair Alfred?"
"Have you read 'Tears, Idle Tears'?"[†] he asked.
"Yes, but you do not there express divine despair."
"My poor friend," he answered, "that was why the despair
Was divine."

Mabel Osborne

YOUR RED BLOSSOMS amid green leaves
Are drooping, beautiful geranium!
But you do not ask for water.
You cannot speak! You do not need to speak—
Everyone knows that you are dying of thirst,
Yet they do not bring water!
They pass on, saying:
"The geranium wants water."
And I, who had happiness to share
And longed to share your happiness;
I who loved you, Spoon River,
And craved your love,
Withered before your eyes, Spoon River—
Thirsting, thirsting,
Voiceless from chasteness of soul to ask you for love,
You who knew and saw me perish before you,
Like this geranium which someone has planted over me,
And left to die.

William H. Herndon

THERE BY THE window in the old house
Perched on the bluff, overlooking miles of valley,
My days of labor closed, sitting out life's decline,
Day by day did I look in my memory,
As one who gazes in an enchantress' crystal globe,
And I saw the figures of the past,
As if in a pageant glassed by a shining dream,
Move through the incredible sphere of time.
And I saw a man arise from the soil like a fabled giant
And throw himself over a deathless destiny,
Master of great armies, head of the republic,
Bringing together into a dithyramb of recreative song
The epic hopes of a people;
At the same time Vulcan† of sovereign fires,
Where imperishable shields and swords were beaten out
From spirits tempered in heaven.
Look in the crystal! See how he hastens on
To the place where his path comes up to the path
Of a child of Plutarch† and Shakespeare.†
O Lincoln, actor indeed, playing well your part,
And Booth,† who strode in a mimic play within the play,
Often and often I saw you,
As the cawing crows winged their way to the wood
Over my house-top at solemn sunsets,
There by my window,
Alone.

Rebecca Wasson

SPRING AND SUMMER, Fall and Winter and Spring,
After each other drifting, past my window drifting!
And I lay so many years watching them drift and counting
The years till a terror came in my heart at times,
With the feeling that I had become eternal; at last
My hundredth year was reached! And still I lay
Hearing the tick of the clock, and the low of cattle
And the scream of a jay flying through falling leaves!
Day after day alone in a room of the house
Of a daughter-in-law stricken with age and gray.
And by night, or looking out of the window by day
My thought ran back, it seemed, through infinite time
To North Carolina and all my girlhood days,
And John, my John, away to the war with the British,
And all the children, the deaths, and all the sorrows.
And that stretch of years like a prairie in Illinois
Through which great figures passed like hurrying horsemen,
Washington,† Jefferson,† Jackson,† Webster,† Clay.†
O beautiful young republic for whom my John and I
Gave all of our strength and love!
And O my John!
Why, when I lay so helpless in bed for years,
Praying for you to come, was your coming delayed?
Seeing that with a cry of rapture, like that I uttered
When you found me in old Virginia after the war,
I cried when I beheld you there by the bed,
As the sun stood low in the west growing smaller and fainter
In the light of your face!

Rutherford McDowell

THEY BROUGHT ME ambrotypes
Of the old pioneers to enlarge.
And sometimes one sat for me—
Some one who was in being
When giant hands from the womb of the world
Tore the republic.
What was it in their eyes?—
For I could never fathom
That mystical pathos of drooped eyelids,
And the serene sorrow of their eyes.
It was like a pool of water,
Amid oak trees at the edge of a forest,
Where the leaves fall,
As you hear the crow of a cock
From a far-off farm house, seen near the hills
Where the third generation lives, and the strong men
And the strong women are gone and forgotten.
And these grand-children and great grand-children
Of the pioneers!
Truly did my camera record their faces, too,
With so much of the old strength gone,
And the old faith gone,
And the old mastery of life gone,
And the old courage gone,
Which labors and loves and suffers and sings
Under the sun!

Hannah Armstrong

I WROTE HIM a letter asking him for old times' sake
To discharge my sick boy from the army;
But maybe he couldn't read it.
Then I went to town and had James Garber,
Who wrote beautifully, write him a letter.
But maybe that was lost in the mails.
So I traveled all the way to Washington.
I was more than an hour finding the White House.
And when I found it they turned me away,
Hiding their smiles. Then I thought:
"Oh, well, he ain't the same as when I boarded him
And he and my husband worked together
And all of us called him Abe, there in Menard."†
As a last attempt I turned to a guard and said:
"Please say it's old Aunt Hannah Armstrong
From Illinois, come to see him about her sick boy
In the army."
Well, just in a moment they let me in!
And when he saw me he broke in a laugh,
And dropped his business as president,
And wrote in his own hand Doug's discharge,
Talking the while of the early days,
And telling stories.†

Lucinda Matlock

I WENT TO the dances at Chandlerville,†
And played snap-out at Winchester.†
One time we changed partners,
Driving home in the moonlight of middle June,
And then I found Davis.
We were married and lived together for seventy years,
Enjoying, working, raising the twelve children,
Eight of whom we lost
Ere I had reached the age of sixty.
I spun, I wove, I kept the house, I nursed the sick,
I made the garden, and for holiday
Rambled over the fields where sang the larks,
And by Spoon River gathering many a shell,
And many a flower and medicinal weed—
Shouting to the wooded hills, singing to the green valleys.
At ninety-six I had lived enough, that is all,
And passed to a sweet repose.
What is this I hear of sorrow and weariness,
Anger, discontent and drooping hopes?
Degenerate sons and daughters,
Life is too strong for you—
It takes life to love Life.

Davis Matlock

SUPPOSE IT IS nothing but the hive:
That there are drones and workers
And queens, and nothing but storing honey—
(Material things as well as culture and wisdom)—
For the next generation, this generation never living,
Except as it swarms in the sun-light of youth,
Strengthening its wings on what has been gathered,
And tasting, on the way to the hive
From the clover field, the delicate spoil.
Suppose all this, and suppose the truth:
That the nature of man is greater
Than nature's need in the hive;
And you must bear the burden of life,
As well as the urge from your spirit's excess—
Well, I say to live it out like a god
Sure of immortal life, though you are in doubt,
Is the way to live it.
If that doesn't make God proud of you,
Then God is nothing but gravitation,
Or sleep is the golden goal.

Herman Altman

DID I FOLLOW Truth wherever she led,
And stand against the whole world for a cause,
And uphold the weak against the strong?
If I did I would be remembered among men
As I was known in life among the people,
And as I was hated and loved on earth,
Therefore, build no monument to me,
And carve no bust for me,
Lest, though I become not a demi-god,
The reality of my soul be lost,
So that thieves and liars,
Who were my enemies and destroyed me,
And the children of thieves and liars,
May claim me and affirm before my bust
That they stood with me in the days of my defeat.
Build me no monument
Lest my memory be perverted to the uses
Of lying and oppression.
My lovers and their children must not be dispossessed of me;
I would be the untarnished possession forever
Of those for whom I lived.

Jennie M'Grew

NOT, WHERE THE stairway turns in the dark,
A hooded figure, shriveled under a flowing cloak!
Not yellow eyes in the room at night,
Staring out from a surface of cobweb gray!
And not the flap of a condor wing,
When the roar of life in your ears begins
As a sound heard never before!
But on a sunny afternoon,
By a country road,
Where purple rag-weeds bloom along a straggling fence,
And the field is gleaned, and the air is still
To see against the sun-light something black
Like a blot with an iris rim—
That is the sign to eyes of second sight...
And that I saw!

Columbus Cheney

THIS WEEPING WILLOW!
Why do you not plant a few
For the millions of children not yet born,
As well as for us?
Are they not non-existent, or cells asleep
Without mind?
Or do they come to earth, their birth
Rupturing the memory of previous being?
Answer! The field of unexplored intuition is yours.
But in any case why not plant willows for them,
As well as for us?

Wallace Ferguson

THERE AT GENEVA[†] where Mt. Blanc[†] floated above
The wine-hued lake like a cloud, when a breeze was blown
Out of an empty sky of blue, and the roaring Rhone
Hurried under the bridge through chasms of rock;
And the music along the cafés was part of the splendor
Of dancing water under a torrent of light;
And the purer part of the genius of Jean Rousseau[†]
Was the silent music of all we saw or heard—
There at Geneva, I say, was the rapture less
Because I could not link myself with the I of yore,
When twenty years before I wandered about Spoon River?
Nor remember what I was nor what I felt?
We live in the hour all free of the hours gone by. *midnight*
Therefore, O soul, if you lose yourself in death,
And wake in some Geneva by some Mt. Blanc,
What do you care if you know not yourself as the you
Who lived and loved in a little corner of earth
Known as Spoon River ages and ages vanished?

Marie Bateson

YOU OBSERVE THE carven hand
With the index finger pointing heavenward.
That is the direction, no doubt.
But how shall one follow it?
It is well to abstain from murder and lust,
To forgive, do good to others, worship God
Without graven images.
But these are external means after all
By which you chiefly do good to yourself.
The inner kernel is freedom,
It is light, purity—
I can no more,
Find the goal or lose it, according to your vision.

Tennessee Claflin Shope

I WAS THE laughing-stock of the village,
Chiefly of the people of good sense, as they call themselves—
Also of the learned, like Rev. Peet, who read Greek
The same as English.
For instead of talking free trade,
Or preaching some form of baptism;
Instead of believing in the efficacy
Of walking cracks, picking up pins the right way,
Seeing the new moon over the right shoulder,
Or curing rheumatism with blue glass,
I asserted the sovereignty of my own soul.
Before Mary Baker G. Eddy[†] even got started
With what she called science I had mastered the "Bhagavad Gita,"
And cured my soul, before Mary
Began to cure bodies with souls—
Peace to all worlds!

Plymouth Rock Joe

WHY ARE YOU running so fast hither and thither
Chasing midges or butterflies?
Some of you are standing solemnly scratching for grubs;
Some of you are waiting for corn to be scattered.
This is life, is it?
Cock-a-doodle-do! Very well, Thomas Rhodes, *rooster*
You are cock of the walk, no doubt.
But here comes Elliott Hawkins,
Gluck, Gluck, Gluck, attracting political followers.
Quah! quah! quah! why so poetical, Minerva,
This gray morning?
Kittie—quah—quah! for shame, Lucius Atherton,
 The raucous squawk you evoked from the throat
Of Aner Clute will be taken up later
By Mrs. Benjamin Pantier as a cry
Of votes for women: Ka dook—dook!
What inspiration has come to you, Margaret Fuller Slack?
And why does your gooseberry eye
Flit so liquidly, Tennesee Claflin Shope?
Are you trying to fathom the esotericism of an egg?
Your voice is very metallic this morning, Hortense Robbins—
Almost like a guinea hen's!
Quah! That was a guttural sigh, Isaiah Beethoven;
Did you see the shadow of the hawk,
Or did you step upon the drumsticks
Which the cook threw out this morning?
Be chivalric, heroic, or aspiring,
Metaphysical, religious, or rebellious,
You shall never get out of the barnyard
Except by way of over the fence
Mixed with potato peelings and such into the trough!†

Imanuel Ehrenhardt

I BEGAN WITH Sir William Hamilton's[†] lectures.
Then studied Dugald Stewart;[†]
And then John Locke[†] on the Understanding,
And then Descartes,[†] Fichte[†] and Schelling,[†]
Kant[†] and then Schopenhauer[†]—
Books I borrowed from old Judge Somers.
All read with rapturous industry
Hoping it was reserved to me
To grasp the tail of the ultimate secret,
And drag it out of its hole.
My soul flew up ten thousand miles,
And only the moon looked a little bigger.
Then I fell back, how glad of the earth!
All through the soul of William Jones[†]
Who showed me a letter of John Muir.[†]

Samuel Gardner

I WHO KEPT the greenhouse,
Lover of trees and flowers,
Oft in life saw this umbrageous elm,
Measuring its generous branches with my eye,
And listened to its rejoicing leaves
Lovingly patting each other
With sweet aeolian whispers.
And well they might:
For the roots had grown so wide and deep
That the soil of the hill could not withhold
Aught of its virtue, enriched by rain,
And warmed by the sun;
But yielded it all to the thrifty roots,
Through which it was drawn and whirled to the trunk,
And thence to the branches, and into the leaves,
Wherefrom the breeze took life and sang.
Now I, an under-tenant of the earth, can see
That the branches of a tree
Spread no wider than its roots.
And how shall the soul of a man
Be larger than the life he has lived?

Dow Kritt

SAMUEL IS FOREVER talking of his elm—
But I did not need to die to learn about roots:
I, who dug all the ditches about Spoon River.
Look at my elm!
Sprung from as good a seed as his,
Sown at the same time,
It is dying at the top:
Not from lack of life, nor fungus,
Nor destroying insect, as the sexton thinks.
Look, Samuel, where the roots have struck rock,
And can no further spread.
And all the while the top of the tree
Is tiring itself out, and dying,
Trying to grow.

William Jones

ONCE IN A while a curious weed unknown to me,
Needing a name from my books;
Once in a while a letter from Yeomans.[†]
Out of the mussel-shells gathered along the shore
Sometimes a pearl with a glint like meadow rue:
Then betimes a letter from Tyndall[†] in England,
Stamped with the stamp of Spoon River.
I, lover of Nature, beloved for my love of her,
Held such converse afar with the great
Who knew her better than I.
Oh, there is neither lesser nor greater,
Save as we make her greater and win from her keener delight.
With shells from the river cover me, cover me.
I lived in wonder, worshipping earth and heaven.
I have passed on the march eternal of endless life.

William Goode

TO ALL IN the village I seemed, no doubt,
To go this way and that way, aimlessly.
But here by the river you can see at twilight
The soft-winged bats fly zig-zag here and there—
They must fly so to catch their food.
And if you have ever lost your way at night,
In the deep wood near Miller's Ford,
And dodged this way and now that,
Wherever the light of the Milky Way shone through,
Trying to find the path,
You should understand I sought the way
With earnest zeal, and all my wanderings
Were wanderings in the quest.

J. Milton Miles

WHENEVER THE PRESBYTERIAN bell
Was rung by itself, I knew it as the Presbyterian bell.
But when its sound was mingled
With the sound of the Methodist, the Christian,
The Baptist and the Congregational,
I could no longer distinguish it,
Nor any one from the others, or either of them.
And as many voices called to me in life
Marvel not that I could not tell
The true from the false,
Nor even, at last, the voice that I should have known.[†]

Faith Matheny

AT FIRST YOU will know not what they mean,
And you may never know,
And we may never tell you:—
These sudden flashes in your soul,
Like lambent lightning on snowy clouds
At midnight when the moon is full.
They come in solitude, or perhaps
You sit with your friend, and all at once
A silence falls on speech, and his eyes
Without a flicker glow at you:—
You two have seen the secret together,
He sees it in you, and you in him.
And there you sit thrilling lest the Mystery
Stand before you and strike you dead
With a splendor like the sun's.
Be brave, all souls who have such visions!
As your body's alive as mine is dead,
You're catching a little whiff of the ether
Reserved for God Himself.

Scholfield Hurley

GOD! ASK ME not to record your wonders,
I admit the stars and the suns
And the countless worlds.
But I have measured their distances
And weighed them and discovered their substances.
I have devised wings for the air,
And keels for water,
And horses of iron for the earth.
I have lengthened the vision you gave me a million times,
And the hearing you gave me a million times,
I have leaped over space with speech,
And taken fire for light out of the air.
I have built great cities and bored through the hills,
And bridged majestic waters.
I have written the Iliad †and Hamlet;†
And I have explored your mysteries,
And searched for you without ceasing,
And found you again after losing you
In hours of weariness—
And I ask you:
How would you like to create a sun
And the next day have the worms
Slipping in and out between your fingers?

Willie Metcalf

I WAS WILLIE METCALF.
They used to call me "Doctor Meyers,"
Because, they said, I looked like him.
And he was my father, according to Jack McGuire.
I lived in the livery stable,
Sleeping on the floor
Side by side with Roger Baughman's bulldog,
Or sometimes in a stall.
I could crawl between the legs of the wildest horses
Without getting kicked—we knew each other.
 On spring days I tramped through the country
To get the feeling, which I sometimes lost,
That I was not a separate thing from the earth.
I used to lose myself, as if in sleep,
By lying with eyes half-open in the woods.
Sometimes I talked with animals—even toads and snakes—
Anything that had an eye to look into.
Once I saw a stone in the sunshine
Trying to turn into jelly.
In April days in this cemetery
The dead people gathered all about me,
And grew still, like a congregation in silent prayer.
I never knew whether I was a part of the earth
With flowers growing in me, or whether I walked—
Now I know.†

Willie Pennington

THEY CALLED ME the weakling, the simpleton,
For my brothers were strong and beautiful,
While I, the last child of parents who had aged,
Inherited only their residue of power.
But they, my brothers, were eaten up
In the fury of the flesh, which I had not,
Made pulp in the activity of the senses, which I had not,
Hardened by the growth of the lusts, which I had not,
Though making names and riches for themselves.
Then I, the weak one, the simpleton,
Resting in a little corner of life,
Saw a vision, and through me many saw the vision,
Not knowing it was through me.
Thus a tree sprang
From me, a mustard seed.

The Village Atheist

YE YOUNG DEBATERS over the doctrine
Of the soul's immortality
I who lie here was the village atheist,
Talkative, contentious, versed in the arguments
Of the infidels.
But through a long sickness
Coughing myself to death
I read the *Upanishads*† and the poetry of Jesus.
And they lighted a torch of hope and intuition
And desire which the Shadow,
Leading me swiftly through the caverns of darkness,
Could not extinguish.
Listen to me, ye who live in the senses
And think through the senses only:
Immortality is not a gift,
Immortality is an achievement;
 And only those who strive mightily
Shall possess it.

John Ballard

IN THE LUST of my strength
I cursed God, but he paid no attention to me:
I might as well have cursed the stars.
In my last sickness I was in agony, but I was resolute
And I cursed God for my suffering;
Still He paid no attention to me;
He left me alone, as He had always done.
I might as well have cursed the Presbyterian steeple.
Then, as I grew weaker, a terror came over me:
Perhaps I had alienated God by cursing him.
One day Lydia Humphrey brought me a bouquet
And it occurred to me to try to make friends with God,
So I tried to make friends with Him;
But I might as well have tried to make friends with the bouquet.
Now I was very close to the secret,
For I really could make friends with the bouquet
By holding close to me the love in me for the bouquet
And so I was creeping upon the secret, but—

Julian Scott

TOWARD THE LAST
The truth of others was untruth to me;
The justice of others injustice to me;
Their reasons for death, reasons with me for life;
Their reasons for life, reasons with me for death;
I would have killed those they saved,
And saved those they killed.
And I saw how a god, if brought to earth,
Must act out what he saw and thought,
And could not live in this world of men
And act among them side by side
Without continual clashes.
The dust's for crawling, heaven's for flying—
Wherefore, O soul, whose wings are grown,
Soar upward to the sun!

Alfonso Churchill

THEY LAUGHED AT me as "Prof. Moon,"
As a boy in Spoon River, born with the thirst
Of knowing about the stars.
They jeered when I spoke of the lunar mountains,
And the thrilling heat and cold,
And the ebon valleys by silver peaks,
And Spica[†] quadrillions of miles away,
And the littleness of man.
But now that my grave is honored, friends,
Let it not be because I taught
The lore of the stars in Knox College,[†]
But rather for this: that through the stars
I preached the greatness of man,
Who is none the less a part of the scheme of things
For the distance of Spica or the Spiral Nebulae;[†]
Nor any the less a part of the question
Of what the drama means.

Zilpha Marsh

AT FOUR O'CLOCK in late October
I sat alone in the country school-house
Back from the road, mid stricken fields,
And an eddy of wind blew leaves on the pane,
And crooned in the flue of the cannon-stove,
With its open door blurring the shadows
With the spectral glow of a dying fire.
In an idle mood I was running the planchette—
All at once my wrist grew limp,
And my hand moved rapidly over the board,
Till the name of "Charles Guiteau"[†] was spelled,
Who threatened to materialize before me.
I rose and fled from the room bare-headed
Into the dusk, afraid of my gift.
And after that the spirits swarmed—
Chaucer,[†] Caesar,[†] Poe[†] and Marlowe,[†]
Cleopatra[†] and Mrs. Surratt[†]—
Wherever I went, with messages,—
Mere trifling twaddle, Spoon River agreed.
You talk nonsense to children, don't you?
And suppose I see what you never saw
And never heard of and have no word for,
I must talk nonsense when you ask me
What it is I see!

James Garber

DO YOU REMEMBER, passer-by, the path
I wore across the lot where now stands the opera house,
Hasting with swift feet to work through many years?
Take its meaning to heart:
You too may walk, after the hills at Miller's Ford
Seem no longer far away;
Long after you see them near at hand,
Beyond four miles of meadow;

And after woman's love is silent,
Saying no more: "I will save you."
And after the faces of friends and kindred
Become as faded photographs, pitifully silent,
Sad for the look which means: "We cannot help you."
And after you no longer reproach mankind
With being in league against your soul's uplifted hands—
Themselves compelled at midnight and at noon
To watch with steadfast eye their destinies;
After you have these understandings, think of me
And of my path, who walked therein and knew
That neither man nor woman, neither toil,
Nor duty, gold nor power
Can ease the longing of the soul,
The loneliness of the soul!

Lydia Humphrey

BACK AND FORTH, back and forth, to and from the church,
With my Bible under my arm
Till I was gray and old;
Unwedded, alone in the world,
Finding brothers and sisters in the congregation,
And children in the church.
I know they laughed and thought me queer.
I knew of the eagle souls that flew high in the sunlight,
Above the spire of the church, and laughed at the church,
Disdaining me, not seeing me.
But if the high air was sweet to them, sweet was the church to me.
It was the vision, vision, vision of the poets
Democratized!

Le Roy Goldman

"WHAT WILL YOU do when you come to die,
If all your life long you have rejected Jesus,
And know as you lie there, He is not your friend?"
Over and over I said, I, the revivalist.
Ah, yes! but there are friends and friends.
And blessed are you, say I, who know all now,
You who have lost ere you pass,
A father or mother, or old grandfather or mother,
Some beautiful soul that lived life strongly,
And knew you all through, and loved you ever,
Who would not fail to speak for you,
And give God an intimate view of your soul,
As only one of your flesh could do it.
That is the hand your hand will reach for,
To lead you along the corridor
To the court where you are a stranger!

Gustav Richter

AFTER A LONG day of work in my hot-houses
Sleep was sweet, but if you sleep on your left side
Your dreams may be abruptly ended.
I was among my flowers where some one
Seemed to be raising them on trial,
As if after-while to be transplanted
To a larger garden of freer air.
And I was disembodied vision
Amid a light, as it were the sun
Had floated in and touched the roof of glass
Like a toy balloon and softly bursted,
And etherealized in golden air.
And all was silence, except the splendor
Was immanent with thought as clear
As a speaking voice, and I, as thought,
Could hear a Presence think as he walked
Between the boxes pinching off leaves,
Looking for bugs and noting values,
With an eye that saw it all:—
"Homer,[†] oh yes! Pericles,[†] good.
Caesar Borgia,[†] what shall be done with it?
Dante,[†] too much manure, perhaps.
Napoleon,[†] leave him awhile as yet.
Shelley,[†] more soil. Shakespeare,[†] needs spraying—"
Clouds, eh!—

Arlo Will

DID YOU EVER see an alligator
Come up to the air from the mud,
Staring blindly under the full glare of noon?
Have you seen the stabled horses at night
Tremble and start back at the sight of a lantern?
Have you ever walked in darkness
When an unknown door was open before you
And you stood, it seemed, in the light of a thousand candles
Of delicate wax?
Have you walked with the wind in your ears
And the sunlight about you
And found it suddenly shine with an inner splendor?
Out of the mud many times
Before many doors of light
Through many fields of splendor,
Where around your steps a soundless glory scatters
Like new-fallen snow,
Will you go through earth, O strong of soul,
And through unnumbered heavens
To the final flame!

Captain Orlando Killion

OH, YOU YOUNG radicals and dreamers,
You dauntless fledglings
Who pass by my headstone,
Mock not its record of my captaincy in the army
And my faith in God!
They are not denials of each other.
Go by reverently, and read with sober care
How a great people, riding with defiant shouts
The centaur of Revolution,
Spurred and whipped to frenzy,
Shook with terror, seeing the mist of the sea
Over the precipice they were nearing,
And fell from his back in precipitate awe
To celebrate the Feast of the Supreme Being.
Moved by the same sense of vast reality
Of life and death, and burdened as they were
With the fate of a race,
How was I, a little blasphemer,
Caught in the drift of a nation's unloosened flood,
To remain a blasphemer,
And a captain in the army?

Jeremy Carlisle

PASSER-BY, SIN beyond any sin
Is the sin of blindness of souls to other souls.
And joy beyond any joy is the joy
Of having the good in you seen, and seeing the good
At the miraculous moment!
Here I confess to a lofty scorn,
And an acrid skepticism.
But do you remember the liquid that Penniwit
Poured on tintypes making them blue
With a mist like hickory smoke?
Then how the picture began to clear
Till the face came forth like life?
So you appeared to me, neglected ones,
And enemies too, as I went along
With my face growing clearer to you as yours
Grew clearer to me.
We were ready then to walk together
And sing in chorus and chant the dawn
Of life that is wholly life.

Joseph Dixon

WHO CARVED THIS shattered harp on my stone?
I died to you, no doubt. But how many harps and pianos
Wired I and tightened and disentangled for you,
Making them sweet again—with tuning fork or without?
Oh well! A harp leaps out of the ear of a man, you say,
But whence the ear that orders the length of the strings
To a magic of numbers flying before your thought
Through a door that closes against your breathless wonder?
Is there no Ear round the ear of a man, that it senses
Through strings and columns of air the soul of sound?
I thrill as I call it a tuning fork that catches
The waves of mingled music and light from afar,
The antennæ of Thought that listens through utmost space.
Surely the concord that ruled my spirit is proof
Of an Ear that tuned me, able to tune me over
And use me again if I am worthy to use.

Judson Stoddard

ON A MOUNTAIN top above the clouds
That streamed like a sea below me
I said that peak is the thought of Buddha,[†]
And that one is the prayer of Jesus,
And this one is the dream of Plato,[†]
And that one there the song of Dante,[†]
And this is Kant[†] and this is Newton,[†]
And this is Milton[†] and this is Shakespeare,[†]
And this the hope of the Mother Church,
And this—why all these peaks are poems,
Poems and prayers that pierce the clouds.
And I said "What does God do with mountains
That rise almost to heaven?"

Russell Kincaid

IN THE LAST spring I ever knew,
In those last days,
I sat in the forsaken orchard
Where beyond fields of greenery shimmered
The hills at Miller's Ford;
Just to muse on the apple tree
With its ruined trunk and blasted branches,
And shoots of green whose delicate blossoms
Were sprinkled over the skeleton tangle,
Never to grow in fruit.
And there was I with my spirit girded
By the flesh half dead, the senses numb,
Yet thinking of youth and the earth in youth,—
Such phantom blossoms palely shining
Over the lifeless boughs of Time.
O earth that leaves us ere heaven takes us!
Had I been only a tree to shiver
With dreams of spring and a leafy youth,
Then I had fallen in the cyclone
Which swept me out of the soul's suspense
Where it's neither earth nor heaven.

Aaron Hatfield

BETTER THAN GRANITE, Spoon River,
Is the memory-picture you keep of me
Standing before the pioneer men and women
There at Concord Church on Communion day.
Speaking in broken voice of the peasant youth
Of Galilee[†] who went to the city
And was killed by bankers and lawyers;
My voice mingling with the June wind
That blew over wheat fields from Atterbury;
While the white stones in the burying ground
Around the Church shimmered in the summer sun.
And there, though my own memories
Were too great to bear, were you, O pioneers,
With bowed heads breathing forth your sorrow
For the sons killed in battle and the daughters
And little children who vanished in life's morning,
Or at the intolerable hour of noon.
But in those moments of tragic silence,
When the wine and bread were passed,
Came the reconciliation for us—
Us the ploughmen and the hewers of wood,
Us the peasants, brothers of the peasant of Galilee—
To us came the Comforter
And the consolation of tongues of flame!

Isaiah Beethoven

THEY TOLD ME I had three months to live,
So I crept to Bernadotte,
And sat by the mill for hours and hours
Where the gathered waters deeply moving
Seemed not to move:
O world, that's you!
You are but a widened place in the river
Where Life looks down and we rejoice for her
Mirrored in us, and so we dream
And turn away, but when again
We look for the face, behold the low-lands
And blasted cotton-wood trees where we empty
Into the larger stream!
But here by the mill the castled clouds
Mocked themselves in the dizzy water;
And over its agate floor at night
The flame of the moon ran under my eyes
Amid a forest stillness broken
By a flute in a hut on the hill.
At last when I came to lie in bed
Weak and in pain, with the dreams about me,
The soul of the river had entered my soul,
And the gathered power of my soul was moving
So swiftly it seemed to be at rest
Under cities of cloud and under
Spheres of silver and changing worlds—
Until I saw a flash of trumpets
Above the battlements over Time.

Elijah Browning

I WAS AMONG multitudes of children
Dancing at the foot of a mountain.
A breeze blew out of the east and swept them as leaves,
Driving some up the slopes...All was changed.
Here were flying lights, and mystic moons, and dream-music.
A cloud fell upon us. When it lifted all was changed.
I was now amid multitudes who were wrangling.
Then a figure in shimmering gold, and one with a trumpet,
And one with a sceptre stood before me.
They mocked me and danced a rigadoon and vanished...
All was changed again. Out of a bower of poppies
A woman bared her breasts and lifted her open mouth to mine.
I kissed her. The taste of her lips was like salt.
She left blood on my lips. I fell exhausted.
I arose and ascended higher, but a mist as from an iceberg
Clouded my steps. I was cold and in pain.
Then the sun streamed on me again,
And I saw the mists below me hiding all below them.
And I, bent over my staff, knew myself
Silhouetted against the snow. And above me
Was the soundless air, pierced by a cone of ice,
Over which hung a solitary star!
A shudder of ecstasy, a shudder of fear
Ran through me. But I could not return to the slopes—
Nay, I wished not to return.
For the spent waves of the symphony of freedom
Lapped the ethereal cliffs about me.
Therefore I climbed to the pinnacle.
I flung away my staff.
I touched that star
With my outstretched hand.
I vanished utterly.
For the mountain delivers to Infinite Truth
Whosoever touches the star!

Webster Ford

DO YOU REMEMBER, O Delphic Apollo,[†]
The sunset hour by the river, when Mickey M'Grew
Cried, "There's a ghost," and I, "It's Delphic Apollo";
And the son of the banker derided us, saying, "It's light
By the flags at the water's edge, you half-witted fools."
And from thence, as the wearisome years rolled on, long after
Poor Mickey fell down in the water tower to his death,
Down, down, through bellowing darkness, I carried
The vision which perished with him like a rocket which falls
And quenches its light in earth, and hid it for fear
Of the son of the banker, calling on Plutus[†] to save me?
Avenged were you for the shame of a fearful heart,
Who left me alone till I saw you again in an hour
When I seemed to be turned to a tree with trunk and branches
Growing indurate, turning to stone, yet burgeoning
In laurel leaves, in hosts of lambent laurel,
Quivering, fluttering, shrinking, fighting the numbness
Creeping into their veins from the dying trunk and branches!
'Tis vain, O youth, to fly the call of Apollo.[†]
Fling yourselves in the fire, die with a song of spring,
If die you must in the spring. For none shall look
On the face of Apollo and live, and choose you must
'Twixt death in the flame and death after years of sorrow,
Rooted fast in the earth, feeling the grisly hand,
Not so much in the trunk as in the terrible numbness
Creeping up to the laurel leaves that never cease
To flourish until you fall. O leaves of me
Too sere for coronal wreaths, and fit alone
For urns of memory, treasured, perhaps, as themes
For hearts heroic, fearless singers and livers—
Delphic Apollo.

The Spooniad

[The late Mr. Jonathan Swift Somers, laureate of Spoon River (see page 88), planned The Spooniad as an epic in twenty-four books, but unfortunately did not live to complete even the first book. The fragment was found among his papers by William Marian Reedy and was for the first time published in Reedy's Mirror of December 18th, 1914.]

The Spooniad [†]

OF JOHN CABANIS' wrath and of the strife
Of hostile parties, and his dire defeat
Who led the common people in the cause
Of freedom for Spoon River, and the fall
Of Rhodes' bank that brought unnumbered woes
And loss to many, with engendered hate
That flamed into the torch in Anarch[†] hands
To burn the court-house, on whose blackened wreck
A fairer temple rose and Progress stood—
Sing, muse, that lit the Chian's[†] face with smiles
Who saw the ant-like Greeks and Trojans[†] crawl
About Scamander,[†] over walls, pursued
Or else pursuing, and the funeral pyres
And sacred hecatombs, and first because
Of Helen[†] who with Paris[†] fled to Troy[†]
As soul-mate; and the wrath of Peleus,[†] son,
Decreed to lose Chryseis,[†] lovely spoil
Of war, and dearest concubine.
                              Say first,
Thou son of night, called Momus,[†] from whose eyes
No secret hides, and Thalia,[†] smiling one,
What bred 'twixt Thomas Rhodes and John Cabanis
The deadly strife? His daughter Flossie, she,
Returning from her wandering with a troop
Of strolling players, walked the village streets,
Her bracelets tinkling and with sparkling rings
And words of serpent wisdom and a smile
Of cunning in her eyes. Then Thomas Rhodes,
Who ruled the church and ruled the bank as well,
Made known his disapproval of the maid;
And all Spoon River whispered and the eyes

Of all the church frowned on her, till she knew
They feared her and condemned.
                                    But them to flout
She gave a dance to viols and to flutes,
Brought from Peoria, and many youths,
But lately made regenerate through the prayers
Of zealous preachers and of earnest souls,
Danced merrily, and sought her in the dance,
Who wore a dress so low of neck that eyes
Down straying might survey the snowy swale
Till it was lost in whiteness.
                              · With the dance
The village changed to merriment from gloom.
The milliner, Mrs. Williams, could not fill
Her orders for new hats, and every seamstress
Plied busy needles making gowns; old trunks
And chests were opened for their store of laces
And rings and trinkets were brought out of hiding
And all the youths fastidious grew of dress;
Notes passed, and many a fair one's door at eve
Knew a bouquet, and strolling lovers thronged
About the hills that overlooked the river.
Then, since the mercy seats more empty showed,
One of God's chosen lifted up his voice:
"The woman of Babylon† is among us; rise,
Ye sons of light and drive the wanton forth!"
So John Cabanis left the church and left
The hosts of law and order with his eyes
By anger cleared, and him the liberal cause
Acclaimed as nominee to the mayoralty
To vanquish A. D. Blood.
                          But as the war
Waged bitterly for votes and rumors flew
About the bank, and of the heavy loans
Which Rhodes' son had made to prop his loss
In wheat, and many drew their coin and left
The bank of Rhodes more hollow, with the talk
Among the liberals of another bank
Soon to be chartered, lo, the bubble burst
'Mid cries and curses; but the liberals laughed

And in the hall of Nicholas Bindle held
Wise converse and inspiriting debate.

High on a stage that overlooked the chairs
Where dozens sat, and where a pop-eyed daub
Of Shakespeare, very like the hired man
Of Christian Dallman, brown and pointed beard,
Upon a drab proscenium outward stared,
Sat Harmon Whitney, to that eminence,
By merit raised in ribaldry and guile,
And to the assembled rebels thus he spake:
"Whether to lie supine and let a clique
Cold-blooded, scheming, hungry, singing psalms,
Devour our substance, wreck our banks and drain
Our little hoards for hazards on the price
Of wheat or pork, or yet to cower beneath
The shadow of a spire upreared to curb
A breed of lackeys and to serve the bank
Coadjutor in greed, that is the question.
Shall we have music and the jocund dance,
Or tolling bells? Or shall young romance roam
These hills about the river, flowering now
To April's tears, or shall they sit at home,
Or play croquet where Thomas Rhodes may see,
I ask you? If the blood of youth runs o'er
And riots 'gainst this regimen of gloom,
Shall we submit to have these youths and maids
Branded as libertines and wantons?"
                                        Ere
His words were done a woman's voice called "No!"
Then rose a sound of moving chairs, as when
The numerous swine o'er-run the replenished troughs;
And every head was turned, as when a flock
Of geese back-turning to the hunter's tread
Rise up with flapping wings; then rang the hall
With riotous laughter, for with battered hat
Tilted upon her saucy head, and fist
Raised in defiance, Daisy Fraser stood.
Headlong she had been hurled from out the hall
Save Wendell Bloyd, who spoke for woman's rights,

Prevented, and the bellowing voice of Burchard.
Then 'mid applause she hastened toward the stage
And flung both gold and silver to the cause
And swiftly left the hall.

                Meantime upstood
A giant figure, bearded like the son
Of Alcmene,[†] deep-chested, round of paunch,
And spoke in thunder: "Over there behold
A man who for the truth withstood his wife—
Such is our spirit—when that A. D. Blood
Compelled me to remove Dom Pedro[†]—"

                      Quick
Before Jim Brown could finish, Jefferson Howard
Obtained the floor and spake: "Ill suits the time
For clownish words, and trivial is our cause
If naught's at stake but John Cabanis' wrath,
He who was erstwhile of the other side
And came to us for vengeance. More's at stake
Than triumph for New England or Virginia.
And whether rum be sold, or for two years
As in the past two years, this town be dry
Matters but little—Oh yes, revenue
For sidewalks, sewers; that is well enough!
I wish to God this fight were now inspired
By other passion than to salve the pride
Of John Cabanis or his daughter. Why
Can never contests of great moment spring
From worthy things, not little? Still, if men
Must always act so, and if rum must be
The symbol and the medium to release
From life's denial and from slavery,
Then give me rum!"

                  Exultant cries arose.
Then, as George Trimble had o'ercome his fear
And vacillation and begun to speak,
The door creaked and the idiot, Willie Metcalf,
Breathless and hatless, whiter than a sheet,
Entered and cried: "The marshal's on his way
To arrest you all. And if you only knew
Who's coming here to-morrow; I was listening

Beneath the window where the other side
Are making plans."
                    So to a smaller room
To hear the idiot's secret some withdrew
Selected by the Chair; the Chair himself
And Jefferson Howard, Benjamin Pantier,
And Wendell Bloyd, George Trimble, Adam Weirauch,
Imanuel Ehrenhardt, Seth Compton, Godwin James
And Enoch Dunlap, Hiram Scates, Roy Butler,
Carl Hamblin, Roger Heston, Ernest Hyde
And Penniwit, the artist, Kinsey Keene,
And E. C. Culbertson and Franklin Jones,
Benjamin Fraser, son of Benjamin Pantier
By Daisy Fraser, some of lesser note,
And secretly conferred.
                    But in the hall
Disorder reigned and when the marshal came
And found it so, he marched the hoodlums out
And locked them up.
                    Meanwhile within a room
Back in the basement of the church, with Blood
Counseled the wisest heads. Judge Somers first,
Deep learned in life, and next him, Elliott Hawkins
And Lambert Hutchins; next him Thomas Rhodes
And Editor Whedon; next him Garrison Standard,
A traitor to the liberals, who with lip
Upcurled in scorn and with a bitter sneer:
"Such strife about an insult to a woman—
A girl of eighteen" —Christian Dallman too,
And others unrecorded. Some there were
Who frowned not on the cup but loathed the rule
Democracy achieved thereby, the freedom
And lust of life it symbolized.

Now morn with snowy fingers up the sky
Flung like an orange at a festival
The ruddy sun, when from their hasty beds
Poured forth the hostile forces, and the streets
Resounded to the rattle of the wheels
That drove this way and that to gather in

The tardy voters, and the cries of chieftains
Who manned the battle. But at ten o'clock
The liberals bellowed fraud, and at the polls
The rival candidates growled and came to blows.
Then proved the idiot's tale of yester-eve
A word of warning. Suddenly on the streets
Walked hog-eyed Allen, terror of the hills
That looked on Bernadotte ten miles removed.
No man of this degenerate day could lift
The boulders which he threw, and when he spoke
The windows rattled, and beneath his brows,
Thatched like a shed with bristling hair of black,
His small eyes glistened like a maddened boar.
And as he walked the boards creaked, as he walked
A song of menace rumbled. Thus he came,
The champion of A. D. Blood, commissioned
To terrify the liberals. Many fled
As when a hawk soars o'er the chicken yard.
He passed the polls and with a playful hand
Touched Brown, the giant, and he fell against,
As though he were a child, the wall; so strong
Was hog-eyed Allen. But the liberals smiled.
For soon as hog-eyed Allen reached the walk,
Close on his steps paced Bengal Mike,† brought in
By Kinsey Keene, the subtle-witted one,
To match the hog-eyed Allen. He was scarce
Three-fourths the other's bulk, but steel his arms,
And with a tiger's heart. Two men he killed
And many wounded in the days before,
And no one feared.
                          But when the hog-eyed one
Saw Bengal Mike his countenance grew dark,
The bristles o'er his red eyes twitched with rage,
The song he rumbled lowered. Round and round
The court-house paced he, followed stealthily
By Bengal Mike, who jeered him every step:
"Come, elephant, and fight! Come, hog-eyed coward!
Come, face about and fight me, lumbering sneak!
Come, beefy bully, hit me, if you can!
Take out your gun, you duffer, give me reason

To draw and kill you. Take your billy out;
I'll crack your boar's head with a piece of brick!"
But never a word the hog-eyed one returned,
But trod about the court-house, followed both
By troops of boys and watched by all the men.
All day, they walked the square. But when Apollo
Stood with reluctant look above the hills
As fain to see the end, and all the votes
Were cast, and closed the polls, before the door
Of Trainor's drug store Bengal Mike, in tones
That echoed through the village, bawled the taunt:
"Who was your mother, hog-eyed?" In a trice
As when a wild boar turns upon the hound
That through the brakes upon an August day
Has gashed him with its teeth, the hog- one
Rushed with his giant arms on Bengal Mike
And grabbed him by the throat. Then rose to heaven
The frightened cries of boys, and yells of men
Forth rushing to the street. And Bengal Mike
Moved this way and now that, drew in his head
As if his neck to shorten, and bent down
To break the death grip of the hog-eyed one;
'Twixt guttural wrath and fast-expiring strength
Striking his fists against the invulnerable chest
Of hog-eyed Allen. Then, when some came in
To part them, others stayed them, and the fight
Spread among dozens; many valiant souls
Went down from clubs and bricks.
                                        But tell me, Muse,
What god or goddess rescued Bengal Mike?
With one last, mighty struggle did he grasp
The murderous hands and turning kick his foe.
Then, as if struck by lightning, vanished all
The strength from hog-eyed Allen, at his side
Sank limp those giant arms and o'er his face
Dread pallor and the sweat of anguish spread.
And those great knees, invincible but late,
Shook to his weight. And quickly as the lion
Leaps on its wounded prey, did Bengal Mike
Smite with a rock the temple of his foe,

And down he sank and darkness o'er his eyes
Passed like a cloud.
               As when the woodman fells
Some giant oak upon a summer's day
And all the songsters of the forest shrill,
And one great hawk that has his nestling young
Amid the topmost branches croaks, as crash
The leafy branches through the tangled boughs
Of brother oaks, so fell the hog-eyed one
Amid the lamentations of the friends
Of A. D. Blood.
             Just then, four lusty men
Bore the town marshal, on whose iron face
The purple pall of death already lay,
To Trainor's drug store, shot by Jack McGuire.
And cries went up of "Lynch him!" and the sound
Of running feet from every side was heard
Bent on the

THE END

Epilogue

(THE GRAVEYARD OF SPOON RIVER. TWO VOICES ARE HEARD BEHIND A SCREEN DECORATED WITH DIABOLICAL AND ANGELIC FIGURES IN VARIOUS ALLEGORICAL RELATIONS. A FAINT LIGHT SHOWS DIMLY THROUGH THE SCREEN AS IF IT WERE WOVEN OF LEAVES, BRANCHES AND SHADOWS.)

FIRST VOICE: A game of checkers?[†]

SECOND VOICE: Well, I don't mind.

FIRST VOICE: I move the Will.[†]

SECOND VOICE: You're playing it blind.

FIRST VOICE: Then here's the Soul.

SECOND VOICE: Checked by the Will.

FIRST VOICE: Eternal Good!

SECOND VOICE: And Eternal Ill.

FIRST VOICE: I haste for the King row.

SECOND VOICE: Save your breath.

FIRST VOICE: I was moving Life.

SECOND VOICE: You're checked by Death.

FIRST VOICE: Very good, here's Moses.[†]

SECOND VOICE: And here's the Jew.

FIRST VOICE: My next move is Jesus.

SECOND VOICE: St. Paul[†] for you!

FIRST VOICE: Yes, but St. Peter[†]—

SECOND VOICE: You might have foreseen—

FIRST VOICE: You're in the King row—

SECOND VOICE: With Constantine![†]

FIRST VOICE: I'll go back to Athens.[†]

SECOND VOICE: Well, here's the Persian.

FIRST VOICE: All right, the Bible.

SECOND VOICE: Pray now, what version?

FIRST VOICE: I take up Buddha.[†]

SECOND VOICE: It never will work.

FIRST VOICE: From the corner Mahomet.[†]

SECOND VOICE: I move the Turk.

FIRST VOICE: The game is tangled; where are we now?

SECOND VOICE: You're dreaming worlds. I'm in the King row.
Move as you will, if I can't wreck you
I'll thwart you, harry you, rout you, check you.

FIRST VOICE:	I'm tired. I'll send for my Son to play.
	I think he can beat you finally—
SECOND VOICE:	Eh?
FIRST VOICE:	I must preside at the stars' convention.
SECOND VOICE:	Very well, my lord, but I beg to mention
	I'll give this game my direct attention.
FIRST VOICE:	A game indeed! But Truth is my quest.
SECOND VOICE:	Beaten, you walk away with a jest.
	I strike the table, I scatter the checkers.

(A rattle of a falling table and checkers flying over a floor.)

Aha! You armies and iron deckers,
Races and states in a cataclysm—
Now for a day of atheism!

(The screen vanishes and BEELZEBUB[†] *steps forward carrying a trumpet, which he blows faintly. Immediately* LOKI[†] *and* YOGARINDRA[†] *start up from the shadows of night.)*

BEELZEBUB:	Good evening, Loki!
LOKI:	The same to you!
BEELZEBUB:	And Yogarindra!
YOGARINDRA:	My greetings, too.
LOKI:	Whence came you, comrade?
BEELZEBUB:	From yonder screen.
YOGARINDRA:	And what were you doing?
BEELZEBUB:	Stirring His spleen.[†]
LOKI:	How did you do it?
BEELZEBUB:	I made it rough
	In a game of checkers.
LOKI:	Good enough!
YOGARINDRA:	I thought I heard the sounds of a battle.
BEELZEBUB:	No doubt! I made the checkers rattle,
	Turning the table over and strewing
	The bits of wood like an army pursuing.
YOGARINDRA:	I have a game! Let us make a man.
LOKI:	My net is waiting him, if you can.
YOGARINDRA:	And here's my mirror to fool him with—
BEELZEBUB:	Mystery, falsehood, creed and myth.
LOKI:	But no one can mold him, friend, but you.
BEELZEBUB:	Then to the sport without more ado.
YOGARINDRA:	Hurry the work ere it grow to day.

BEELZEBUB: I set me to it. Where is the clay?
              (He scrapes the earth with his hands and begins to model.)
BEELZEBUB: Out of the dust,
              Out of the lime,
              A little rust,
              And a little lime.
              Muscle and gristle,
              Mucin, stone
              Brayed with a pestle,
              Fat and bone.
              Out of the marshes,
              Out of the vaults,
              Matter crushes
              Gas and salts.
              What is this you call a mind,
              Flitting, drifting, pale and blind,
              Soul of the swamp that rides the wind?
              Jack-o'-lantern, here you are!
         Dream of heaven, pine for a star,
         Chase you brothers to and fro,
         Back to the swamp at last you'll go.
         Hilloo! Hilloo!

THE VALLEY: Hilloo! Hilloo!
              (BEELZEBUB *in scraping up the earth turns out a skull.*)

BEELZEBUB: Old one, old one.
              Now ere I break you
              Crush you and make you
              Clay for my use,
              Let me observe you:
              You were a bold one
              Flat at the dome of you,
              Heavy the base of you,
              False to the home of you,
              Strong was the face of you,
              Strange to all fears.
              Yet did the hair of you
              Hide what you were.
              Now to re-nerve you—

(He crushes the skull between his hands and mixes it with the clay.)
    Now you are dust,
    Limestone and rust.
    I mold and I stir
    And make you again.

THE VALLEY: Again? Again?
    (In the same manner BEELZEBUB *has fashioned several figures,*
  standing them against the trees.)

LOKI: Now for the breath of life. As I remember
    You have done right to mold your creatures first,
    And stand them up.

BEELZEBUB: From gravitation
    I make the will.

YOGARINDRA: Out of sensation
    Comes his ill.
    Out of my mirror
    Springs his error.
    Who was so cruel
    To make him the slave
    Of me the sorceress, you the knave,
    And you the plotter to catch his thought,
    Whatever he did, whatever he sought?
    With a nature dual
    Of will and mind,
    A thing that sees, and a thing that's blind.
    Come! to our dance! Something hated him
    Made us over him, therefore fated him.
        (They join hands and dance.)

LOKI: Passion, reason, custom, rules,
    Creeds of the churches, lore of the schools,
    Taint in the blood and strength of soul.
    Flesh too weak for the will's control;
    Poverty, riches, pride of birth,
    Wailing, laughter, over the earth,
    Here I have you caught again,
    Enter my web, ye sons of men.

YOGARINDRA: Look in my mirror! Isn't it real?
    What do you think now, what do you feel?
    Here is a treasure of gold heaped up;

Here is wine in the festal cup.
Tendrils blossoming, turned to whips,
Love with her breasts and scarlet lips.
Breathe in the nostrils.

BEELZEBUB: Falsehood's breath,
Out of nothingness into death
Out of the mold, out of the rocks,
Wonder, mocker, paradox!
Soaring spirit, groveling flesh,
Bait the trap, and spread the mesh.
Give him hunger, lure him with truth,
Give him the iris hopes of Youth.
Starve him, shame him, fling him down,
Whirled in the vortex of the town.
Break him, age him, till he curse
The idiot face of the universe.
Over and over we mix the clay,—
What was dust is alive to-day.

THE THREE: Thus is the hell-born tangle wound
Swiftly, swiftly round and round.

BEELZEBUB: *(Waving his trumpet.)*
You live! Away!

ONE OF THE FIGURES: How strange and new!
I am I, and another, too.

ANOTHER FIGURE: I was a sun-dew's leaf, but now
What is this longing?—

ANOTHER FIGURE: Earth below
I was a seedling magnet-tipped
Drawn down earth—

ANOTHER FIGURE: And I was gripped
Electrons in a granite stone,
Now I think.

ANOTHER FIGURE: Oh, how alone!

ANOTHER FIGURE: My lips to thine. Through thee I find
Something alone by love divined!

BEELZEBUB: Begone! No, wait. I have bethought me, friends;
Let's give a play.
    (He waves his trumpet.)
To yonder green rooms go.
  (The figures disappear.)

YOGARINDRA: Oh, yes, a play! That's very well, I think,
                     But who will be the audience? I must throw
                     Illusion over all.

LOKI: And I must shift
                     The scenery, and tangle up the plot.

BEELZEBUB: Well, so you shall! Our audience shall come
                     From yonder graves.

*(He blows his trumpet slightly louder than before. The scene
changes. A stage arises among the graves. The curtain is down,
concealing the creatures just created, illuminated halfway up by
the spectral lights. BEELZEBUB stands before the curtain.)*

BEELZEBUB: *(A terrific blast of the trumpet.)*
                     Who-o-o-o-o-o!

*(Immediately there is a rustling as of the shells of
grasshoppers stirred by a wind; and hundreds of the dead,
including those who have appeared in the Anthology, hurry to the
sound of the trumpet.)*

A VOICE: Gabriel!† Gabriel!

MANY VOICES: The Judgment day!

BEELZEBUB: Be quiet, if you please
                     At least until the stars fall and the moon.

MANY VOICES: Save us! Save us!

*(Beelzebub extends his hands over the audience with a
benedictory motion and restores order.)*

BEELZEBUB: Ladies and gentlemen, your kind attention
                     To my interpretation of the scene.
                     I rise to give your fancy comprehension,
                     And analyze the parts of the machine.
                     My mood is such that I would not deceive you,
                     Though still a liar and the father of it,
                     From judgment's frailty I would retrieve you,
                     Though falsehood is my art and though I love it.
                     Down in the habitations whence I rise,
                     The roots of human sorrow boundless spread.
                     Long have I watched them draw the strength that lies
                     In clay made richer by the rotting dead.
                     Here is a blossom, here a twisted stalk,
                     Here fruit that sourly withers ere its prime;
                     And here a growth that sprawls across the walk,
                     Food for the green worm, which it turns to slime

The ruddy apple with a core of cork
Springs from a root which in a hollow dangles,
Not skillful husbandry nor laborious work
Can save the tree which lightning breaks and tangles.
Why does the bright nasturtium scarcely flower
But that those insects multiply and grow,
Which make it food, and in the very hour
In which the veined leaves and blossoms blow?
Why does a goodly tree, while fast maturing,
Turn crooked branches covered o'er with scale?
Why does the tree whose youth was not assuring
Prosper and bear while all its fellows fail?
I under earth see much. I know the soil.
I know where mold is heavy and where thin.
I see the stones that thwart the plowman's toil,
The crooked roots of what the priests call sin.
I know all secrets, even to the core,
What seedlings will be upas, pine or laurel;
It cannot change howe'er the field's worked o'er.
Man's what he is and that's the devil's moral.
So with the souls of ensuing drama
They sprang from certain seed in certain earth.
Behold them in the devil's cyclorama,
Shown in their proper light for all they're worth.
Now to my task: I'll give an exhibition
Of mixing the ingredients of spirit.

(He waves his hand.)

Come, crucible, perform your magic mission,
Come, recreative fire, and hover near it!
I'll make a soul, or show how one is made.

(He waves his wand again. Parti-colored flames appear.)

This is the woman you shall see anon!

(A red flame appears.)

This hectic flame makes all the world afraid:
It was a soldier's scourge which ate the bone.
His daughter bore the lady of the action,
And died at thirty-nine of scrofula.
She was a creature of a sweet attraction,
Whose sex-obsession no one ever saw.

(A purple flame appears.)

Lo! this denotes aristocratic strains
Back in the centuries of France's glory.
(*A blue flame appears.*)
    And this the will that pulls against the chains
Her father strove until his hair was hoary.
Sorrow and failure made his nature cold,
He never loved the child whose woe is shown,
And hence her passion for the things which gold
Brings in this world of pride, and brings alone.
The human heart that's famished from its birth
Turns to the grosser treasures, that is plain.
Thus aspiration fallen fills the earth
With jungle growths of bitterness and pain
Of Celtic,[†] Gallic[†] fire our heroine!
Courageous, cruel, passionate and proud.
False, vengeful, cunning, without fear o' sin.
A head that oft is bloody, but not bowed.
Now if she meet a man—suppose our hero,
With whom her chemistry shall war yet mix,
As if she were her Borgia[†] to his Nero,[†]
'Twill look like one of Satan's little tricks!
However, it must be. The world's great garden[†]
Is not all mine. I only sow the tares.
Wheat should be made immune, or else the Warden
Should stop their coming in the world's affairs.
But to our hero! Long ere he was born
I knew what would repel him and attract.[†]
Such spirit mathematics, fig or thorn,
I can prognosticate before the fact.
(*A yellow flame appears.*)
    This is a grandsire's treason in an orchard
Against a maid whose nature with his mated.
(*Lurid flames appear.*)
    And this his memory distrait and tortured,
Which marked the child with hate because she hated.
Our heroine's grand dame was that maid's own cousin—
But never this our man and woman knew.
The child, in time, of lovers had a dozen,
Then wed a gentleman upright and true.
And thus our hero had a double nature:

One half of him was bad, the other good.
The devil must exhaust his nomenclature
To make this puzzle rightly understood.
But when our hero and our heroine met
They were at once attracted, the repulsion
Was hidden under Passion, with her net
Which must enmesh you ere you feel revulsion.
The virus coursing in the soldier's blood,
The orchard's ghost, the unknown kinship 'twixt
        them,
Our hero's mother's lovers round them stood,
Shadows that smiled to see how Fate had fixed them.
This twain pledge vows and marry, that's the play.
And then the tragic features rise and deepen.
He is a tender husband. When away
The serpents from the orchard slyly creep in.
Our heroine, born of spirit none too loyal,
Picks fruit of knowledge—leaves the tree of life.
Her fancy turns to France corrupt and royal,
Soon she forgets her duty as a wife.
You know the rest, so far as that's concerned,
She met exposure and her husband slew her.
He lost his reason, for the love she spurned.
He prized her as his own—how slight he knew her.

(He waves a wand, showing a man in prison cell.)

Now here he sits condemned to mount the gallows—
He could not tell his story—he is dumb.
Love, says your poets, is a grace that hallows,
I call it suffering and martyrdom.
The judge with pointed finger says, "You killed her."
Well, so he did—but here's the explanation;
He could not give it. I, the drama-builder,
Show you the various truths and their relation.

(He waves his wand.)

Now, to begin. The curtain is ascending,
They meet at tea upon a flowery lawn.
Fair, is it not? How sweet their souls are blending—
The author calls the play "Laocoon"[†]

A VOICE: Only an earth dream.
ANOTHER VOICE: With which we are done.

	A flash of a comet
	Upon the earth stream.
ANOTHER VOICE:	A dream twice removed,
	A spectral confusion
	Of earth's dread illusion.
A FAR VOICE:	These are the ghosts
	From the desolate coasts.
	Would you go to them?
	Only pursue them.
	Whatever enshrined is
	Within you is you.
	In a place where no wind is,
	Out of the damps,
	Be ye as lamps.
	Flame-like aspire
	To me alone true,
	The Life and the Fire

BEELZEBUB, LOKI *and* YOGARINDRA *vanish. The phantasmagoria fades out. Where the dead seemed to have assembled, only heaps of leaves appear. There is the light as of dawn. Voices of Spring.)*

FIRST VOICE:	The springtime is come, the winter departed,
	She wakens from slumber and dances light-hearted.
	The sun is returning,
	We are done with alarms,
	Earth lifts her face burning,
	Held close in his arms.
	The sun is an eagle
	Who broods o'er his young,
	The earth is his nursling
	In whom he has flung
	The life-flame in seed,
	In blossom desire,
	Till fire become life,
	And life become fire.
SECOND VOICE:	I slip and I vanish,
	I baffle your eye;
	I dive and I climb,
	I change and I fly.
	You have me, you lose me,
	Who have me too well,

	Now find me and use me—
	I am here in a cell.
THIRD VOICE:	You are there in a cell?
	Oh, now for a rod
	With which to diving you—
SECOND VOICE:	Nay, child, I am God.
FOURTH VOICE:	When the waking waters rise from their beds of snow, under the hill,

In little rooms of stone where they sleep when icicles
    reign,
The April breezes scurry through woodlands, saying
    "Fulfill!
Awaken roots under cover of soil—it is Spring
    again."

Then the sun exults, the moon is at peace, and voices
Call to the silver shadows to lift the flowers from
    their dreams.
And a longing, longing enters my heart of sorrow, my
    heart that rejoices
In the fleeting glimpse of a shining face, and her hair
    that gleams.
I arise and follow alone for hours the winding way by
    the river,
Hunting a vanishing light, and a solace for joy too
    deep.
Where do you lead me, wild one, on and on forever?
Over the hill, over the hill, and down to the meadows
of sleep.

THE SUN: Over the soundless depths of space for a hundred
    million miles
Speeds the soul of me, silent thunder, struck from a
    harp of fire.
Before my eyes the planets wheel and a universe
    defiles,
I but a luminant speck of dust upborne in a vast
    desire.
What is my universe that obeys me—myself
    compelled to obey

A power that holds me and whirls me over a path
    that has no end?
And there are my children who call me great, the
    giver of life and day,
Myself a child who cry for life and know not whither
    I tend.
A million million suns above me, as if the curtain of
    night
Were hung before creation's flame, that shone
    through the weave of the cloth,
Each with its worlds and worlds and worlds crying
    upward for light,
For each is drawn in its course to what?—as the
    candle draws the moth.

THE MILKY WAY: Orbits unending,
    Life never ending,
    Power without end.

A VOICE: Wouldst thou be lord,
    Not peace but a sword.
    Not heart's desire—
    Ever aspire.
    Worship thy power,
    Conquer thy hour,
    Sleep not but strive,
    So shalt thou live.

INFINITE DEPTHS: Infinite Law,
    Infinite Life.

Glossary

Due to the number of epitaphs in *Spoon River Anthology*, the Glossary and Vocabulary have been arranged in alphabetical order to allow for more efficient navigation; however, *The Hill* is in the beginning, as it appears in the text, and *The Spooniad* and the *Epilogue* are located at the end.

The Hill

The Hill – This poem, different in both length and form from the others in *Spoon River Anthology*, sets the tone for the book. Basically, it serves as an introduction. In "The Hill," Masters develops the concept that this book is a collection of epitaphs from the small town of Spoon River, Illinois, that represents different ways of living and dying, and, despite evil, wealth, or innocence, everyone is equal in death and they are all "sleeping on the hill."

A

Armstrong, Hannah

Menard – a city in Illinois

"I wrote him…and telling stories." – This epitaph tells the story of Armstrong's attempts to receive a discharge from the army for her son.

Arnett, Justice

"…why do you torture me with leaves…" – As Justice lay dying, papers showered around him, "like a deck of cards," he describes. These pieces of paper represented his life and the accomplishments he made over the years. The papers also represented the thoughts of dying people, when evaluating their lives. This can be a negative experience because one has the tendency to be over critical of his or her decisions, experiences, and accomplishments.

Atheist, The Village

Upanishads – a collection of texts believed to date as far back as 500 B.C.; they cover the theology and teachings of ancient Hinduism.

Atherton, Lucius

"When my moustache…dregs of life." – Atherton, who previously had been a cad and a womanizer, felt discarded and useless before he died. His earlier life as a lover is overshadowed by what he has become.

B

Bartlett, Ezra

ecstatic vision – a state of religious inspiration

celestial outposts – a possible reference to the community of Heaven

Bennett, Hon. Henry
"It never came...clownish soul!" – This is another sad commentary on the way people misconstrue life and love.

Bindle, Nicholas
probated – After a person dies, the estate is examined by a probate court to determine whether or not it can be left to a descendent; if no descendent or will is present, the law appoints a representative to handle the distribution of the estate.

Blood, A.D.
"If you in the...unholy pillow?" – Note the sarcasm in this epitaph and who Blood believes the true sinners really are.

Bone, Richard
"When I first...to hide it." – It is interesting to note how Richard was in charge of engraving the tombstones and how skeptical he was of the words he carved; yet the reader assumes they accurately portray that person, unlike Richard, who has been "party" to the lies.

Branson, Caroline
Raphael – an archangel in the Old Testament
St. Francis – (c.1182 – 1226), a very influential Roman Catholic friar

Brown, Jim
Dom Pedro – an alcoholic drink made with ice cream and whisky
"Turkey in the straw" – a popular American folk song
"There is a fountain filled with blood" – a popular hymn written by William Cooper
Concord – a small village in Morgan County, Illinois
"skipping the light fantastic" – a phrase used to describe a joyful, happy time; it is also a cliché for "dancing."
"passing the plate" – a reference to passing the collection plate during church services
Pinafore – the Gilbert and Sullivan opera, *H. M. S. Pinafore*

Brown, Sarah
Nirvana – paradise, heaven

Burke, Robert Southey
Robert Southey – This person's name refers to a former poet laureate of England, Robert Southey (1774 – 1843).

Burleson, John Horace
"...to enrich my art..." – John Horace Burleson moved to the city to "enrich" his craft of writing; instead, he neglected his craft for another, more lucrative occupation—banking. He longed for the immortality that comes with writing a famous piece of literature; instead, he died a stranger.

Matthew Arnold – (1822 – 1888), a British poet and literary critic who wrote about morals and religious doubt—he wrote in his *The Study of Poetry* that he believed poetry would, one day, replace religion.

Emerson – Ralph Waldo Emerson (1803 – 1882), a philosopher and writer of Transcendental ideals, which focuses on Nature, the divine nature of the individual, the importance of simplicity, and the inborn good nature of all humankind

"Roll on, thou deep and dark blue Ocean, roll!" – a line from Lord George Gordon Byron's "Childe Harold's Pilgrimage"; Byron is considered to be one of the greatest Romantic poets, and Burleson regrets that he never wrote a line of poetry as impressive as this of Byron's.

Butler, Roy
Ipava; Table Grove – two villages in Illinois

C
Cabanis, Flossie
"East Lynne" – a novel by Henry Woods about a woman who disgraces her family by running away with a murderer, only to return years later disguised as a nurse to be near her fatally-ill son
Duse – a possible reference to Elenora Duse (1858 – 1924), an Italian actress who toured the U.S.

Cabanis, John
Plato's lofty guardians – a class of rulers Plato created in his *Republic*

Calhoun, Henry C.
Furies – from Greek mythology, three goddesses who seek out and punish mortals for crimes
Fates – three mythological goddesses who are said to control human destiny
Atropos – one of the three Fates; she is in charge of "cutting the thread of life"

Chicken, Ida
Chautauqua – an educational exhibit geared toward adults; these exhibits traveled from town to town with lectures, plays, and musical performances

Church, John M.
Church – His name proves to be ironic when compared with his actions; John Church was not a holy man, rather, he was a man of deception and cold-heartedness.
"...the rats devoured...in my skull!" – John's occupation caused him to become cold and deceptive—he no longer cared about the well-being of others, instead, he was only concerned with making more money for the "Q" company.

Churchill, Alfonso
Spica – [Latin] "ear of grain"; Spica is typically associated with the constellation Virgo, as it is the brightest star in this constellation, and, consequently, it is one of the brightest stars in the sky.
Knox College – a liberal arts college in Illinois

Spiral Nebulae – a galaxy with a spiral structure

Clapp, Homer
"Often Aner Clute...like a man." – Note Homer's connection to both Lucius Atherton
and Aner Clute.

Clark, Nellie
"...the village agreed...he deserted me..." – Nellie's poem is written in a secretive
fashion, but her story is relatively easy to decipher if read carefully. These final
lines exhibit the judgmental nature of the town, and how powerful the town's
influence truly is. It is unclear how Nellie died.

Clute, Aner
"Suppose a boy steals...makes the boy what he is." – Aner's life was judged and
criticized; she felt labeled by her community as a disgraced woman because she
fell for Lucius Atherton. With her experience, then, she finds parallels with story
of a the young boy who stole the apples. His act essentially defined who he was,
regardless of who he *really* was. Therefore, Aner is stating that the way her com-
munity perceived her, indisputably made her who she was because she could not
be seen any differently, no matter what she did to try to change its perceptions.

Compton, Seth
Volney's "Ruins" – a reference to Constantin de Volney's (1757 – 1820) famous con-
troversial book, *Les Ruines; ou Méditation sur les révolutions des empires* (1791).
Les Ruines focused on religious skepticism and became very popular in France,
England, and the United States.
Butler's "Analogy" – a reference to Joseph Butler's (1692 – 1752) *The Analogy of
Religion, Natural and Revealed, to the Constitution and Course of Nature* (1736).
Butler's *Analogy* directly attacked Deism, which is a belief that was founded on
the notion that after God created the universe, He left it to develop and progress
naturally, without His influence.
"Faust" – a reference to Johan Wolfgang von Goethe's (1749 – 1832) poem based
on the legend of a German doctor who sold his soul to the devil in exchange for
necromantic powers
"Evangeline" – a reference to Henry Wadsworth Longfellow's (1807 – 1882) poem
about an Acadian woman's search for her husband after they were separated
during the Great Expulsion (an ordered "population transfer"; Acadians—early
French settlers in Canada—were forced to leave Nova Scotia).
"That no one knows...what is false." – Compton wants Spoon River to see the error
it committed: By selling its library, the town closed itself to knowledge.

D
Davidson, Robert
"Remember the acorn..." – Interestingly, British women once carried acorns with
them everywhere they went because it was said that acorns would delay the aging
process. Davidson could be referring to this folklore in reference to his own
desire for immortality.

Dement, Silas
Joliet – a city in Illinois; a prison in Illinois

Dobyns, Batterton
Mackinac – a region in the Michigan area
Manitoba – a province in central Canada

Dye, Shack
"...And you didn't...Spoon River." – Dye, a black man, had suffered from the jokes
   that Spoon River residents played on him, but realizes that the others were just
   as gullible as he was.

E
Ehrenhardt, Imanuel
Sir William Hamilton – (1788 – 1856), a Scottish philosopher and history profes-
   sor
Dugald Stewart – (1753 – 1828), a Scottish philosopher and mathematics professor
John Locke – (1632 – 1704), an English philosopher best known for his *Essay
   Concerning Human Understanding* (1690)
Descartes – Rene Descartes (1596 – 1650), the French philosopher and mathemati-
   cian famous for his quote, "I think, therefore I am"
Fichte – Johann Gottlieb Fichte (1762 – 1814), a German philosopher who argued
   that practical reason was the basis for all knowledge and humanity
Schelling – Friedrich Wilhelm Joseph von Schelling (1775 – 1854), a German ideal-
   ist philosopher
Kant – See note: *Kant* in "Ippolit Konovaloff" glossary.
Schopenhauer – Arthur Shopenhauer (1788 – 1860), a German philosopher
William Jones – (1746 – 1794), a British linguist and jurist who studied and was
   renowned for his understanding of Asian languages
John Muir – (1838 – 1914), a Scottish naturalist known as "The Father of the
   National Parks System"
"I began with...John Muir." – Note that despite reading all these different philoso-
   phers, Ehrenhardt is most impressed by John Muir, who admired nature above
   all else.

F
Ferguson, Wallace
Geneva – a city in Switzerland
Mt. Blanc – a mountain in the French Alps
Jean Rousseau – (1644 – 1699) a famous French composer and viol player

Fluke, Willard
Cleopatra – (69 B.C. – 30 B.C.), Queen of Egypt, known for her beauty
"My little girl...blind!" – His daughter being born blind is symbolic. First, her
   blindness reminded Fluke of his wife and her illness, which is why Fluke says he
   committed infidelity initially. In addition, his daughter's blindness allowed her to
   be ignorant of her father's misery, which also added to his guilt.

"My wife lost...all is blackness!" – Willard Fluke's epitaph is a clear illustration of how he lived the last part of his life—in fear, full of guilt, and miserable. After he and his friends cheated on their wives, Fluke noticed how the following years "Death claimed [his friends] all in some hideous form" undoubtedly to punish them for the sin they committed. Fluke fearfully anticipated his death. Metaphorically, it can be said that Fluke's death was slow and painful, as the thought of it consumed his life. He found religion, and Jesus spoke to him, telling him how to find forgiveness within himself and God. Fluke's heart was too weak with guilt, and it failed.

Foote, Searcy

Proudhon – Pierre-Joseph Proudhon (1809 – 1865) was a French anarchist (see note: *anarchists* in Carl Hamblin's glossary) who believed human development would eventually abolish all necessity for a government.

"I poured...till she died.—" – In one of the most revealing epitaphs, Foote seems to be so proud of fooling the residents of Spoon River that he admits to a murder. Previously, no one had even known that a crime took place.

Ford, Webster

O Delphic Apollo – an allusion to the oracle of Apollo, located in Delphi

Plutus – the god of wealth

Apollo – the god of the sun

French, Charlie

Vicksburg – a city in western Mississippi; the site of a Civil War battle.

G

Garrick, Amelia

"You have succeeded...complete triumph." – It is unclear whom Amelia is speaking to with her poem, but it is possible that the woman from New York is her sister or a close friend whom Amelia helped over the years, with no gratitude in return. It is obvious Amelia is hurt and angry in the beginning of the poem, but toward the end, even though her words are still a bit harsh, it is as though Amelia has come to peace with her role in life and the knowledge that the woman in New York will never be in complete control because of Amelia's help and guidance.

Godbey, Jacob

libertarians – people who are in favor of limiting the power of and maximizing the rights of the individual

Goodpasture, Jacob

Fort Sumter – Built between the years 1829 and 1860 in Charleston, South Carolina, this fort was where the Civil War began.

"thirty million souls being bound together" – Goodpasture is referring to how he is now connected to the millions of souls who have gone before him.

Transfiguration – a Christian belief in which Jesus is transformed into gleaming light; this event marks the end of Christ's public life (Matthew 17:1-6).

golden eagles – a symbol Goodpasture uses for the United States

"**Forgive the blindness of the departed owl**" – After his death, Goodpasture finally realized how beneficial the war was for his beloved country.

Graham, Magrady
Altgeld – John Peter Altgeld (1847 – 1902) was the governor of Illinois in 1893.
"**Did they bring...a dancer...**" – a biblical reference; Salome, a sensual dancer, asked Herod, the ruler of Galilee, to bring her John the Baptist's head.

Gray, George
"**It is a boat...yet afraid.**" – George Gray was a safe man; he never took risks, and, therefore, he never truly lived. The boat on his tomb is a symbol for his life. George's life, like the boat, was idle; his sails were turned in, hiding from the wind. The irony of having a boat symbolize idleness is that George had the possibility to live a full life—he could have opened his sails and glided through life, enjoying everything it had to offer, but he chose the safer route.

Gustine, Dorcas
Dorcas – the biblical name of a woman whose kindness and love helped the poor; although the Dorcas in *Spoon River Anthology* did not help the poor, it is ironic that her name literally means "good woman," yet she was disliked by her entire community.
Spartan boy – a reference to the story of a boy who let a wolf eat him without complaining; the young boy was praised for his bravery by his fellow Spartans, but, because of her outspoken nature, Dorcas is offended by the boy's silence and believes it is an act of cowardice.
"**silence poisons the soul**" – Although Dorcas was ridiculed for being outspoken, she has no regrets. She is leaving her loved ones, her community, and all those who will read her epitaph with a message and advice on how to live life. She is now content in her grave because she said everything that came to her mind while she was alive. Silence can be dangerous, and she hopes everyone will heed her warning.

H
Hainsfeather, Barney
"**But to be buried here—*ach!***" – The mistake of being buried in a Christian cemetery seems to evoke disgust.

Hamblin, Carl
Anarchists – people in favor of having no government
"**I saw a beautiful...wore the bandage.**" – This section of the epitaph, an editorial written in the Spoon River newspaper, is a scathing indictment of the traditional portrayal of "Lady Justice," who is usually pictured as being blind to anything other than facts in a case. The incident in Chicago refers to a historical incident, The Haymarket Affair, which took place in 1886. the hangings of anarchists took place three years later.

Hatfield, Aaron
Galilee – an area in northern Israel

Henry, Chase
"Take note...in shame." – This comment relates to the general theme that the way people live their lives is not directly related to how they are perceived after they die.

Herndon, William H.
Vulcan – in Roman mythology, the god of fire, volcanoes, and craftsmanship
Plutarch – (46 – 120), a Greek author and philosopher famous for writing biographies of many influential figures
Shakespeare – William Shakespeare (1564 – 1616), a famous playwright and poet who was influential during the Elizabethan era
Booth – most likely an allusion to John Wilkes Booth (1838 – 1865)

gbie, Archibald
Apollo – a reference to the handsome son of Zeus; the son god (see note: *Apollo* in Webster Ford's glossary)
Lincoln – a reference to Abraham Lincoln (1809 – 1865)

Hoheimer, Knowlt
staid – The use of the spelling in this instance is significant. Obviously, the spelling should be *stayed*, but with the use of *staid* the word takes on several different meanings. Most notably, *staid* refers to permanence, being fixed in one spot, which directly relates to Knowlt wishing he had not joined the army. The word *staid* also refers to *dignity*—serious or grave dignity—that would have given him the strength he needed to stay in Spoon River and suffer the consequence of theivery, rather than running away, (and in Lydia Puckett's epitaph it is made clear that he was running from a relationship as well).
Missionary Ridge – a series of hills that stretch from southeast Tennessee to northwest Georgia; Missionary Ridge was the site of an important Civil War battle.
Pro Patria – [Latin] "For (one's) country"; the fact that Knowlt does not know the meaning of this phrase emphasizes that his joining the army had nothing to do with his love for his country.

Holden, Barry
"And I killed her." – This epitaph is interesting because Barry never mentions how he died; his purpose in the epitaph, though, is to admit the sin he committed while he was living. There are other poems that also admit guilt or sin in an attempt to redeem the dead in the afterlife.

Hookey, Sam
"Whereupon Brutus sprang...killed me." – Brutus, the lion, is most likely an allusion to Shakespeare's *Julius Caesar*, in which Cassius influences Brutus to think that Caesar is an oppressive tyrant and an arrogant leader. As a result, Brutus agrees to join the conspiracy against Caesar. Brutus kills Caesar, just as Brutus, the lion, kills Sam in response to the beating.
Robespierre – an allusion to Maximilien Robespierre (1758 – 1794), a leading political figure during the French Revolution; Robespierre's radical and violent actions became known as the Reign of Terror. His ruling tactics worked against him,

causing a mutiny and ultimately, his murder. Robespierre's ghostly presence at Sam's death is symbolic of Sam's treatment toward the lions. The lions turned on Hookey, and murdered him because of his treatment toward them, which is very similar to Robespierre's experience.

Houghton, Jonathan
Atterbury – a city in Illinois

Howard, Jefferson
Calvinists – followers of John Calvin (1509 – 1564), a theologian who believed in an all-knowing God, the grace of God, and that salvation is only granted to those whom God selects

Hurley, Scholfield
Iliad – an ancient Greek poem by Homer that chronicled the Trojan War
Hamlet – a tragic poem by William Shakespeare (see note: *Shakespeare* in William H. Herndon's glossary)

J
Jack, Blind
"And all we fiddlers...fall of Troy." – Jack is referring to Homer, the blind author of the *Iliad*. The *Iliad* is the story of the Battle of Troy. Fiddlers were said to idolize Homer for his story-telling abilities, as fiddlers were also known for their story telling. Jack also relates to Homer on a more personal level because of their blindness.

Joe, Plymouth Rock
"Why are you...into the trough!" – Note the hostile tone of this epitaph; rather than speak of his life, his death or confess his sins, Plymouth Rock Joe seems to be judging the others in Spoon River, warning them (or threatening them) to remind them that their existence will end in death also, and they should act accordingly.

Johnson, Voltaire
William Wordsworth – (1770 – 1850), a famous English poet

Jones, Fiddler
"Toor-a-Loor" – a popular Irish song
"The earth keeps...single regret." – Jones is one of the few people buried in the cemetery who have no regrets about life.

Jones, Franklin
"Made it look more like a chicken." – Note the irony in Franklin Jones' gravestone with a chicken engraved on it—his gravestone will forever show his failure in life.
"Save that...from the first!" – Note the comparison Jones expresses here: People are holy only because they know that they will die.

Jones, "Indignation"

"...mired in a bog...it was a meadow..." – Note the pun in this statement. The literal definition of *mire* is *to get caught up in* or *to get delayed*—this is true for "Indignation" Jones, as he was *caught up* in being a carpenter; the use of *bog*, which means *to hinder* or *slow*, adds weight to his statement. In addition, *mires* and *bogs* are also types of swamps or areas of muddy waters, which would also *slow* someone's progress or *delay* him or her in some way, which is "Indignation" Jones' pun: As he strolled through life, as if it were a meadow, he was slowed down by the swamps and mud he traversed through on his way.

Jones, Minerva

"I am Minerva...so for life!" – There is a strong hint in this poem that Minerva died because of having to abort her pregnancy ("..."Butch" Weldy / Captured me after a brutal hunt. / He left me to my fate..."), which is confirmed in Doctor Meyers' and Mrs. Meyers' epitaph (see note: *"...Minerva...she died—"* in Doctor Meyers glossary, and also see note: *"He had broken...divine."* in Mrs. Meyers glossary).

Jones, William

Yeomans – a reference to either Edward Youmans (1821 – 1887) or William Youmans (1838 – 1901), both editors of *Popular Science Monthly*, a magazine

Tyndall – John Tyndall (1820 – 1893), an Irish-born, English physicist famous for his work with gases and radiant heat

Judge, The Circuit

Nemesis – a reference to the goddess of justice or revenge from Greek mythology

K

Karr, Elmer

"What but the...rest with Jesus." – Note the connection between Tom Merritt, Mrs. Merritt, and Elmer Karr.

Keene, Jonas

"Why did Albert...Ere he was sixty?" – Both Jonas and Albert are connected in that they each envied the other's lifestyle. These two poems are perfect examples of the cliché, "the grass is always greener..." Jonas was able to see the good in Albert's life that Albert just could not see; and, Albert could see only how good Jonas' life was. Neither man could see the good in his own life.

Keene, Kinsey

Social Purity Club – a reference to the movement during the late 1880s that concentrated on controlling and containing all forms of adultery, prostitution, and pornography. The movement focused primarily on protecting adolescent girls.

Cambronne – Pierre Jacques Etienne, viscomte Cambronne (1770 – 1842) was a French general who fought and was wounded during the Battle of Waterloo.

Napoleon – Napoleon Bonaparte (1769 – 1821), Emperor of France

Maitland – It is uncertain if this allusion is historically accurate or a fictitious character made specifically for Keene's epitaph; the name "Maitland" was originally a French place-name, that, when translated to English, probably meant something like "inhospitable" in Old French.

Kessler, Mrs.

Grant's Memoirs – a possible reference to Ulysses S. Grant's (1822 – 1885) memoirs

"Mr. Kessler, you know...washed and ironed." – Note the housekeeping metaphor that runs throughout this epitaph.

Knapp, Nancy

"...we never had any peace...struck the granary." – The unfortunate irony in this poem is that the farm was purchased with inheritance money with the hope of a better future; instead, the cattle died and the crops failed.

Decatur – an Illinois city, east of Springfield

Konovaloff, Ippolit

Odessa – a city in Texas

Spencer – most likely a reference to Herbert Spencer (1820 – 1903), an English philosopher who followed Charles Darwin's theories of evolution; Spencer is most famous for his ten-volume publication *Synthetic Philosophy*.

Kant – Immanuel Kant (1724 – 1804), a German, idealist philosopher

L

Lively, Judge Selah

"Suppose you stood...hard for them?" – In an effort to find forgiveness, Judge Lively justifies his actions although they were committed for revenge.

M

M'Cumber, Daniel

Niles – a city in Illinois

Fourierist – a system developed in the 19th century by Charles Fourier who wanted to design small, self-sufficient, self-sustaining communities

"Why, Mary...of your robe!" – Daniel's epitaph is a confession and a plea for forgiveness. He addresses Mary McNeely in the first line. He desires her forgiveness because he knew how much she suffered because of him. He admits to his weaknesses of falling into temptation and learned that he did not deserve Mary's love or her tears.

McFarlane, Widow

loom – a machineWidow McFarlane used frequently; an implement used to weave thread into cloth.

"And you weave...figures in gold and purple." – Note the extended metaphor with references to weaving all the way through the epitaph.

McGee, Fletcher

"She took my...me for life." – Note the comparison between Fletcher's and Ollie's epitaphs: They both blame the other for their unhappiness.

McGuire, Jack

Peoria – a city in northwest Illinois

"They would have...read and write." – Note the reference to The Town Marshal's epitaph regarding prohibition and political corruption.

McNeely, Mary
"Passer-by...Eternal peace!" – Mary writes how her life, once filled with joy and
love, became lonesome and full of sorrow at the loss of her love. She searched her
soul that was lost when her "beloved one withdraws itself from [her] soul..." It
was difficult for her to move on because she spent everyday watching her father
wallow in his own sorrow, never moving on, and never experiencing happiness
again. Through death, though, Mary has finally found her soul and can now rest
in peace.

McNeely, Washington
Ann Arbor – an educational center at the University of Michigan
Rockford – a college for women in Illinois; few women at the time would have
been given a college education. Whatever McNeely was able to give his children
did not matter—they all had major problems in life and seemed to have been
unhappy.

Malloy, Father
Peter the Rock – a reference to Cephas, Jesus' name for St. Peter; the word *cephas* is
Aramaic for "rock" and Greek for "Peter."

Marsh, Zilpha
Charles Guiteau – Charles Julius Guiteau (1840 – 1882), the American lawyer who
assassinated President James Garfield on July 2, 1881
Chaucer – Geoffry Chaucer (c. 1340 – 1400), the English poet famous for writing
The Canterbury Tales
Caesar – most likely a reference to Julius Caesar (101 B.C. – 44 B.C.), the Roman
emperor who was assassinated by a group of conspirators
Poe – Edgar Allan Poe (1809 – 1849), an American author most famous for his clas-
sic poem "The Raven"
Marlowe – Christopher Marlowe (1564 – 1593), an English playwright and poet
Cleopatra – (69 B.C. – 30 B.C.), the Queen of Egypt known for her astounding
beauty
Mrs. Surratt – Mary Eugenia Surratt (1820 – 1865) was a widow who was involved
in the conspiracy to assassinate Abraham Lincoln.

Marshal, The Town
Prohibitionists – a group of individuals who advocated outlawing alcohol

Matlock, Lucinda
Chandlerville – a city in Illinois
Winchester – a city in Illinois

Merritt, Mrs.
Joliet – a prison in Illinois

Metcalf, Willie
"I was Willie Metcalf...Now I know." – This is an unique epitaph because of how
Willie viewed his life. For his entire life, he was treated as an animal, forced to

sleep on the floor next to a dog, working and becoming close with the horses, and even befriending toads and snakes. Only the animals would look him in the eye. Secretly, Willie longed for that respect from his community. Was he one with Nature or one with man? The epitaph ends with the enlightened statement: "Now I know." Is Metcalf content believing he was part of nature because he had no connection with his human community, or did he finally realize that he was a man who walked the earth with others despite the bad treatment he endured?

Meyers, Doctor
"...Minerva...she died—" – Doctor Meyers' epitaph adds to the allusion found in Minerva Jones' epitaph that she needed to abort her pregnancy (see note: *"I am Minerva...so for life!"* in Minerva Jones' glossary).

Meyers, Mrs.
"He had broken...divine." – With her explanation of her husband's attempt to help Minerva, Mrs. Meyers confirms further the actions that took place that night, with her suggestion that the act went against divine law.
"He protested...his commandments." – Note that Mrs. Meyers' epitaph is primarily about her husband, not herself.

Micure, Hamlet
Euripides – (c.480 – 406 B.C.), a Greek playwright
"Tears, Idle Tears" – a poem by Alfred Tennyson (1809 – 1892)

Miles, J. Milton
"Whenever the Presbyterian...I should have known." – Miles is stating a conclusion that many epitaphs reach: There is no difference among the various religions.

Miller, Julia
"I took morphine..." – this reference to morphine could be an indication of a possible suicide

Moir, Alfred
Mason City – a city in Illinois
"...the book in a window...over and over?" – Masters is referring to an ornately decorated copy of Percy Bysshe Shelley's poetry. Masters makes a few other autobiographical comments throughout *Spoon River Anthology.*

N
Nutter, Isa
Peoria – a city in Illinois, north of Springfield

O
Otis, John Hancock
John Hancock – (1737 – 1793), one of the signers of the Declaration of Independence.
"to the manner born" – a reference to *Hamlet,* it means "born to nobility and wealth" here, but in Shakespeare's play, it means "accustomed to."

P

Pantier, Mrs. Benjamin

"Wordsworth's 'Ode' " – an allusion to William Wordsworth (1770 – 1850), a famous English poet and his ode "Intimations of Immortality"

Pantier, Rueben

Rue de Rivoli – a famous street in Paris, named for one of Napoleon's first victories at the battle of Rivoli against the Austrian army in 1797

Peet, Rev. Abner

"I had no...waste paper." – Rev. Peet refers to his congregation as his "beloved flock"; he respected them, but learned after his death that some members of the community did not respect him as he thought they did. Rev. Peet thought he had meant more to the congregation.

Puckett, Lydia

"Knowlt Hoheimer...is a woman." – Lydia's epitaph focuses on Knowlt rather than her own life, which indicates that Lydia was more concerned with Knowlt than herself. In addition, there is no cause of death for Lydia; but this is the case with many of the epitaphs.

Purkapile, Roscoe

"She loved me...I was right." – This epitaph and the one that follows, Mrs. Purkapile, are two more that show both sides of a situation in two different lights.

Putt, Hod

"Here I lie...side by side." – In the opening epitaph, Masters successfully sets the scene for the entire *Spoon River Anthology*. It is based in a small town, early in the twentieth century; the inhabitants are simple people, and "Hod Putt" sets the tone of irony and the unpredictability of fate.

R

Reece, Mrs. George

"And all through the wisdom...the honor lies.'" – a quote by Alexander Pope (1688 – 1744), an English poet

Rhodes, Ralph

will-o'-the-wisp of women – A will-o'-the-wisp is a type of inexplicable light seen at night in fields; the term is also used when describing delusions or hallucinations. Rhodes may refer to the women he chased as such because they were never attainable, and would not have provided him with any enjoyment anyway.

Richter, Gustav

Homer – (c. 900 B.C. – c. 850 B.C.), a Greek poet famous for his two epic poems, the *Odyssey* and the *Iliad* (see *"And all we fiddlers...fall of Troy."* in Blind Jack's glossary)

Pericles – (c. 495 B.C. – 429 B.C.), an Athenean general best known for initiating the construction of the Parthenon

Caesar Borgia – [*Cesare Borgia*] (c. 1475 – 1507), an Italian military leader and politician known and feared for his cruelty; Borgia became the model for *The Prince*, Niccolo Machiavelli's (1469 – 1527) most renowned publication that analyzes political figures and advises future leaders on the art of obtaining power through deception and tyranny.

Dante –Dante Alighieri (1265 – 1321), an Italian poet most famous for writing *The Divine Comedy*, a story of the journey through Hell; it is also widely know as "Dante's *Inferno*."

Napoleon – See note: *Napoleon* in Kinsey Keene's glossary.

Shelley – Percy Bysshe Shelley (1792 – 1822), a well-known Romantic poet (see note: *Percy Bysshe Shelley* in Percy Bysshe Shelley's glossary)

Shakespeare – See note: *Shakespeare* in William H. Herndon's glossary.

Robbins, Hortense

Baden-Baden – a city in Germany that had a spring, which was known for its supposed healing propertiees

Ross, Thomas, Jr.

"This I saw...brother's ambition." – Thomas Ross' story of the cliff-swallow and the snake and the irony that follows is a metaphor used to illustrate the irony in his own life. The mother bird represents Thomas Ross, Jr.; he evidently rose above his figurative predators and survived a difficult situation despite his low ranking, only to become a victim of his brother, who, undoubtedly desired success in life so badly that he would turn his back on his own family.

Russian Sonia

Weimar – a city in Germany

passée – [French] passed

Rutledge, Anne

"With malice...for all." – This quote is from Lincoln's Second Inaugural Address.

Anne Rutledge – (c.1813 – 1835), Abraham Lincoln's supposed fiancée; she died suddenly from a severe fever. Lincoln's love for Anne was recorded in a biography, but his later wife, Mary Todd Lincoln, claimed that the story was false.

S

Schrœder the Fisherman

Bernadotte – a village in Illinois

Sersmith the Dentist

Battle Hymn of the Republic – a hymn written about American patriotism during the Civil War (1861 – 1865) by Julia Ward Howe

Whitney's cotton gin – a reference to Eli Whitney's (1765 – 1825) cotton gin, which he had patented in 1794. The gin made processing cotton easier and more efficient.

Sharp, Percival

Elagabalus – (204 – 222), a Roman emperor who is remembered because of his eccentric behavior and his unconventional religious views

Arimaspi – inhabitants of northern Scythia; Greek writers believed that the Arimaspi had only one eye in the center of their foreheads.

Shaw, "Ace"

"Ace" – This character's name is symbolic of the uncertainty of life and the risks involved in every decision or act. Ace was very much a gambler; therefore, his name, depending on the game, could represent a high card or a low card.

"Seest thou a man...stand before Kings!" – a quote from the Bible (Proverbs, chapter 22:29)

Shelley, Percy Bysshe

Percy Bysshe Shelley – (1792 – 1822), a Romantic poet who may have influenced Masters' poetry. Shelley himself was cremated, and his remains were buried in the Protestant Cemetery in Rome. This Spoon River inhabitant was obviously named after the famous poet, hence, "ashes of my namesake".

pyramid of Caius Cestius – This pyramid is located near a Protestant Church in Rome. Cestius was one of the few priests of a great religious order called *Septemviri epulonum*. The fact that he was buried there is ironic because of Shelley's atheistic tendencies, which caused his expulsion from the University of Oxford.

Shope, Tennessee Claflin

Mary Baker G. Eddy – (1821 – 1910), the founder of the Christian Scientist Church
"Bhagavad Gita" – a sacred Hindu text

Sibley, Mrs.

"My secret: Under...never find." – It is obvious that Mrs. Sibley is a secretive woman; however, she claims to know the secrets of others. It is known from Amos Sibley's epitaph, that his wife committed adultery; therefore, the "mound" Mrs. Sibley mentions can take on several meanings. The first meaning of the "mound" could be that she became pregnant through one of her affairs and died before anyone found out. The second meaning could suggest that when Mrs. Sibley became pregnant through her affair, she aborted the pregnancy; therefore, no one found out. Another meaning could be simply that Mrs. Sibley has taken all of her secrets to the grave. A third

Siever, Conrad

northern-spy – a type of apple that ripens late in the season

Simmons, Walter

"Octoroon" – a popular play that opened in 1859

Slack, Margaret Fuller

Margaret Fuller – This character is named for the Transcendentalist writer and feminist, Margaret Fuller (1810 – 1850)

George Eliot – the pen name for Mary Ann Evans (1819 – 1880), a famous, English novelist

"**Hear me...of life!**" – For Margaret, having a family ruined her chance of becoming the writer she aspired to be.

Smith, Louise
"**Do not let the will...your soul...**" – Note the extended gardening metaphor that runs throughout this poem. Louise must have had a great regard and respect for nature.

Soldiers, Many
Milton – John Milton (1608 – 1674), an English poet known for his epic poem *Paradise Lost* (1667)

"**The idea danced...with Milton's Poems.**" – This epitaph differs from most in this anthology because it represents a group. These soldiers longed to be a part of something that would benefit their country, serve the people and places they loved, and protect the land that was theirs, even if it cost their lives. These men were leading "A dream of duty to country or to God," with pride and valor. Only after their deaths do they realize their strength did not come from weaponry and wrath, but from life. For the soldiers, life should have been their dream; they can see, through Nature, how powerful, courageous, and strong Life can be when it is lived with fervor: "But not a cell in all the tree / Knew aught save that it thrilled with life,..."

Somers, Jonathan Swift
Jonathan Swift – (1667 – 1745), author of *Gulliver's Travels* and *A Modest Proposal*

Somers, Judge
Blackstone – Sir William Blackstone (1723 – 1780) was an English jurist who is famed for writing "Commentaries on the Laws of England," which was the most thorough body of text on English law.

Coke – Sir Edward Coke (1552 – 1634), an English lawyer who served as chief justice of the Court of Common Pleas

Justice Breese – Sydney Breese (1800 – 1878) was an attorney for the Illinois Circuit Court from 1822 to 1826, and later he served as Justice for the Supreme Court of Illinois until 1842. He was elected Senator of Illinois in 1843, and then became chief justice of the Illinois Supreme Court in 1873.

Sparks, Emily
"**Where is my boy...but light!**" – Emily Sparks writes of the students she adopted as her own. One student in particular touched her heart, and this epitaph illustrates how she wished she knew what happened to him. She describes him as a "spirit aflame," which suggests that he had a wild or impulsive nature, probably a very appealing and charismatic characteristic to Emily. Her prayer for him also suggests that he may have been headed down the wrong moral path, which is depicted in Rueben Pantier's epitaph when he is with a "black-eyed cocotte." She tried to sway him, teaching him of "the beautiful love of Christ." Now that she's dead, Emily hopes that that boy found religion without losing the fire (a pun Emily's last name, "sparks") that burned within him.

Spears, Lois

Fluke – Note the irony in Lois Spears' maiden name and her unlucky affliction.

"With an instinct as sure as sight" – Lois' epitaph is also didactic in the sense that she did not let her hardship bring her down—she made the best of what she was given and still maintained a happy and fulfilling life.

Standard, W. Lloyd Garrison

W. Lloyd Garrison – This name probably comes from William Lloyd Garrison (1805 – 1879), a famous anti-slavery leader

Ingersoll – Robert G. Ingersoll (1833 – 1899), a famous orator who influenced Edgar Lee Masters.

abolitionist – a person who advocated getting rid of slavery

Stoddard, Judson

Buddha – Siddhartha Gautama (c. 536 B.C. – c. 483 B.C.), a religious figure and founder of Buddhism; Buddha is also called the "enlightened one."

Plato – (428 B.C. – 347 B.C.), a famous Greek philosopher

Dante – See note: *Dante* in Gustav Richter's glossary

Kant – Seen note: *Kant* in Ippolit Konovaloff's glossary

Newton – possibly an allusion to Sir Isaac Newton (1642 – 1727), an important figure in modern physics and astronomy; he formulated explanations of gravity, the laws of nature, and planetary motion among many others.

Milton – See note: *Milton* in Many Soldiers' glossary

Shakespeare – See note: *Shakespeare* in William H. Herndon's glossary.

T

Tanner, Robert Fulton

Robert Fulton – It is possible, but uncertain, that this character is named for Robert Fulton (1765 – 1815), who is generally considered the inventor of steam-powered ships. Robert Fulton was also a well-known inventor and artist, as well as an engineer.

"If a man…misery bores him." – This entire epitaph is littered with literary elements. The extended metaphor of humans as rats, just waiting for their dying day, runs the length of the poem. The personification of Life indicates that Fulton seems to have felt cheated. The "bait" he speaks of is obviously temptation, both physical and monetary, but Fulton concludes by saying that his life meant nothing if all he did was work and wait for "the monstrous ogre Life."

Taylor, Deacon

"I belonged…*Spiritus frumenti*." – another instance of private versus public behavior influencing people's perceptions

"*Spiritus frumenti*" – [Latin] "Fermented Spirits"

Theodore the Poet

Theodore the Poet – Masters claimed that he wrote this poem for the American novelist, Theodore Dreiser (1871 – 1945), in honor of Dreiser's influence.

Thornton, English

Valley Forge – Located in northwest Philadelphia, Valley Forge was the official head-quarters of General Washington's army from 1777 – 1778 during the American Revolution

Black Hawk – (1767 – 1838), the leader of the Native American Sauk tribe who was driven out of Illinois in 1831

Starved Rock – a steep cliff overlooking the Illinois River

Throckmorton, Alexander

"Genius is wisdom and youth." – Note the tone and style of this short epitaph. Alexander's wisdom and sorrow are expressed clearly—he regrets not having taken the time to get to know the world around him. By the time he realized the importance of "the mountains," he was too tired and old to fully appreciate them, as he would have long ago. Instead, his youth consisted of flying through different places as quickly as possible to do as much as he could—he didn't take the time to appreciate what he saw.

Todd, Eugenia

"Till perfect freedom...glad in the morning!" – Eugenia Todd describes her life as a constant pain, like a toothache. She was obviously unhappy, although, she never states exactly why. With her death, she is free, and she uses freedom as a metaphor for death.

Trevelyan, Thomas

Ovid – (43 B.C. – c.18 A.D.), a famous Roman poet

"...the sorrowful...Procne a swallow..." – In Greek mythology, Tereus was in love with his wife's sister Philomela; he raped Philomela, then cut out her tongue and held her captive to ensure that she would not reveal the crime to anyone. Tereus then told his wife, Procne, that her sister was dead. Secretly, Philomela wove a tapestry full of pictures telling the story of what had happened and had it sent to Procne. Once Procne received the tapestry, she killed her son Itys and fed him to Tereus. When Tereus found out what Procne did, he tried to kill both sisters, but the gods intervened and turned all three characters into birds. Tereus became a bird (hoopoe), Philomela was changed to a swallow, and Procne became a nightingale that sings a song of mourning for her dead son Itys.

Trimble, George

Henry George – (1839 – 1897), a member of the Democratic party who proposed that each state fully tax the usage of land and get rid of all other taxes

Peerless Leader – Masters is referring to William Jennings Bryan (1860 – 1925) who was an Illinois-born Democratic leader as well as the Secretary of State. When Trimble mentions "free-silver," he is referring to Bryan's "Cross of Gold" speech in which Bryan advocated the use of free-silver. The Free Silver Movement began when large amounts of silver were found in the Western United States. The movement aimed to produce unlimited coinage of silver.

"she ruined me" – a didactic element that seems to convey a message about taking responsibility for one's own actions

radicals – members of a political party that desire governmental change in an extreme fashion; a radical reform would be an extreme change of a government policy. **conservatives** – members of a political party who desire no change from the government; conservatives are concerned with maintaining the current order.

Tutt, Oaks

Pontius Pilate – the Roman governor who ordered Jesus' crucifixion
"What is Truth?" – Pilate asks Jesus this question, according to John 18:38

U

Unknown, The

Hades – the land of the dead, according to Greek mythology

W

Wasson, John

"If Harry Williams...from mine!" – Note how the patriotism felt by Williams is contrasted with Wasson's hatred of the flag.

Wasson, Rebecca

Washington – George Washington (1732 – 1799)
Jefferson – Thomas Jefferson (1743 – 1826)
Jackson – Andrew Jackson (1767 – 1845)
Webster – probably a reference to Noah Webster (1758 – 1843), who was responsible for publishing *An American Dictionary of the English Language* in 1828
Clay – This reference has two possibilities: It could be a reference to Cassius Marcellus Clay (1810 – 1903) who was an abolitionist and politician. It could also be a reference to Cassius' direct relative Henry Clay (1777 – 1852), "the Great Compromiser," a politician who advocated the Missouri Compromise.

Wertman, Elsa

"...as my secret began to show." – another case of a woman in Spoon River having been taken advantage of by a man and becoming pregnant out of wedlock
"But—at political rallies...That's my son." – In Hamilton Greene's epitaph, it is ironic that he has died, never knowing his birth mother, but being completely happy and satisfied with his life.

Whitney, Harmon

"Like Byron's did..." – another reference to Lord Byron (see note: *"Roll on, thou deep and dark blue Ocean, roll!"* in John Horace Burleson's glossary)

Wiley, Rev. Lemuel

"...none is treasured...Blisses from divorce..." – Note how Wiley's understanding of his intervention in the divorce is the direct opposite of the opinion of Mrs. Charles Bliss, two poems earlier.

William and Emily

"There is something...love itself!" – This is the only epitaph written for two people in one. This couple, obviously in love, was blinded and could not see society's contradictions around them. Their love protected them from every evil, allowed them to live their lives happily, and let them end their mortal lives together, so their love would live on for all eternity. Their love unified them, which is why they had a single epitaph, because they were one with each other.

Williams, Dora

Champs Élysées – [French] "Elysian Fields"; a thoroughfare in Paris, France

Campo Santo – [Italian] a cemetery

Columbus – a reference to Christopher Columbus (1451 – 1506), the Italian explorer credited with discovering the New World

"*Contessa Navigato / Implora eternal quiete*." – [Latin] "*Countess Navigato, ask for everlasting peace.*"

Williams, Mrs.

"Mother of Dora...her rearing." – Mrs. Williams was blamed for her daughter's disappearance and judged by the community, but Dora's greed (and greedy husband) led Dora to drink from a poisoned cup. The officials in Spoon River were focused on judging and restricting the townspeople in an effort to make Spoon River a well-respected place. In actuality, they focused on trivial judgments and changes that created misery, animosity, and hatred among many inhabitants.

Wilmans, Harry

Tagalogs – the natives of the Philippines

Manila – the capital of the Philippines

Y

Yee Bow

Yee Bow – The name of this character is a play on words because Yee Bow tells of how the members of Spoon River tried to force him to change his religious beliefs—in other words, they asked him to bow down to the beliefs of the community, hence "Yee Bow." Note that this is the first instance of overt racism in the community.

Confucius – (551 B.C. – 479 B.C.) a wise Chinese philosopher whose teachings were followed and became the basis of Chinese education and law

Pekin – the former name of Beijing, the capital of China

Z

Zoll, Perry

The Spooniad

The Spooniad – an epic poem describing the political conflicts of the town (conservatives vs. liberals)

Anarch – a monarch, ruler

Chian – a native of Chios, an island in the Aegean Sea

Trojans – inhabitants of Troy

Scamander – a river in Turkey

Helen – Zeus' daughter, regarded as the most beautiful woman in the world

Paris – the prince of Troy who fell in love with Helen (see note: *Helen*) and fled with her; this event sparked the Trojan War.

Troy – an ancient, Asian city

Peleus – Achilles' father

Chryseis – a woman kidnapped by Agamemnon in the *Iliad*; her father called on Apollo for help. Apollo inflicted the Greek army with a plague until Chryseis was released.

Momus – the god of ridicule in Greek mythology

Thalia – the Muse of comedy

Babylon – an ancient city in Mesopotamia; Babylon's Hanging Gardens known as one of the 7 wonders of the world

Alcmene – In Greek mythology, Alcmene had an affair with Zeus and gave birth to Hercules

Dom Pedro – See note: *Dom Pedro* in Jim Brown's glossary

Bengal Mike – Bengal is an area in India; this character may have been from there and acquired this nickname upon moving to Spoon River.

<u>Epilogue</u>

"A game of checkers?" – The following game of checkers is a metaphor for religions that are constantly fighting for a position above the others. Imagine the checkerboard with each game piece representative of a particular religion. Note each piece's placement and movement across the board.

the Will – a reference to Free Will among all humans

Moses – a Biblical figure who is the prophet responsible for parting the Red Sea, bringing people the Ten Commandments, and leading the Israelites out of Egypt

St. Paul – the apostle who converted to Christianity and became a missionary to spread Christian faith

St. Peter – one of the twelve apostles; St. Peter is noted first in the Gospels, and he is known as the first bishop of Rome.

Constantine – (272 – 337), a Roman general who eventually became emperor; Constantine converted to Christianity and was a major advocate for ceasing Christian persecution.

Athens – the capital of Greece

Buddha – See note: *Buddha* in Judson Stoddard's glossary.

Mahomet – [*Muhammad*] (c.570 – c.632), a religious figure, the founder of Islam; Mahomet converted many to Muslim, and his divine revelations were recorded by his followers in what is now known as the Koran.

Beelzebub – Satan

Loki – an evil god from Norse mythology who constantly caused mischief and uproar

Yogarindra – It is uncertain what the definite origin of this character is; however, Yogarindra could be a foil, created to emphasize the actions of Beezlebub and Loki. The etymology of the name is unclear, as it could also represent another mythological figure.

"Stirring His spleen" – Because "His" is capitalized, it suggests that Beelzebub is referring to the Christian God. The spleen was once thought to be associated with melancholy and irritability.

Gabriel – a Biblical figure (also mentioned in the Koran; see note: *Mahomet*) who announced Jesus' conception, birth, and the divine mission of Mary. In addition, Christians believe that Gabriel will sound the trumpet on Judgment Day.

 Celtic – referring to the Celts; originally Celts occupied central and western Europe, the British Isles, Briton, and Gaul.

Gallic – referring to inhabitants of Gaul, an ancient area in France

Borgia – See note: *Caesar Borgia* in Gustav Richter's glossary .

Nero – (37 – 68), a Roman emperor known for his fierce cruelty

world's great garden – an allusion to the Garden of Eden

"...I knew...attract." – referring to man being easily tempted to commit sins

"Laocoon" – a legend in Greek mythology of the Trojan priest, Laocoon, who was killed by two sea serpents because he warned the Trojans of the danger of accepting the wooden horse presented by the Greeks

Vocabulary

The Hill
brothel – an illegal establishment used for prostitution
thwarted – hindered, stifled
venerable – valued, respected

A
Arnett, Harold
abysm – an abyss

Arnett, Justice
concede – to admit, acknowledge (usually reluctantly)
docket – a file or list of documented statements or things to be done; in this instance, it appears to be a file of all the accomplishments Justice had throughout his life.
sleight – skillfully, dexterously

Atheist, The Village
doctrine – rules or principles of belief (religious)
infidels – people who have no religious beliefs

Atherton, Lucius
dregs – the lowest part, the leftover residue
knave – a crafty person (usually, a dishonest person)

B
Ballard, John
resolute – firm

Barker, Amanda
portals – entrances
proclaim – to declare, announce
slew – past tense of *slay*, killed

Barrett, Pauline
decennial – a ten year anniversary
rapture – extreme joy, ecstasy

Bartlett, Ezra
chaplain – a member of the clergy
divinity – godliness
exhorter – a person who argues certain points

Beethoven, Isaiah
agate – a type of quartz
battlements – an exterior wall built around the top of a castle for additional protection

Bennett, Hon. Henry
anon – presently

ardor – love, passion
malice – hatred, cruelty

Bindle, Nicholas
acquittal – being judged as 'not guilty' of a crime

Bloyd, Wendell P.
blasphemy – swearing against religion
statute – a law, decree
wretched – miserable, pitiful

Bone, Richard
epitaph – the inscription on a tombstone

Branson, Caroline
annihilated – destroyed
canticle – a song or chant (usually from the Bible)
prescient – foresight
trysting – a meeting place
voluptuous – well-developed

Brown, Jim
cantata – a musical performance using text from the Bible

Brown, Sarah
broods – meditates, focuses, worries
rapturous – joyous, ecstatic
whip-poor-will – a type of nocturnal bird
wrought – created

Browning, Elijah
ethereal – heavenly
pinnacle – a peak; the highest point
rigadoon – a type of rapid-paced dance
sceptre – [*scepter*] a staff
wrangling – arguing

Burke, Robert Southey
celluloid – a colorless and flammable material used in making photograph film
fealty – faithfulness
lavished – poured
smelted – melted

Butler, Roy
varlet – an attendant, servant

C
Cabanis, Flossie
enthralled – captivated
kindred spirits – soul mates; best friends

pathos – a feeling of pity or sympathy

<u>Cabanis, John</u>
girdled – surrounded

<u>Calhoun, Granville</u>
smote – cursed, tormented

<u>Calhoun, Henry C.</u>
admonitions – advice, warnings

<u>Campbell, Calvin</u>
arbutus – a type of evergreen tree
elixirs – remedies, cures to restore health
jessamine – [*jasmine*] a fragrant flower used for aromatherapy
Jimpson – a weed used as a medicinal herb
wistaria – [*wisteria*] a type of vine with blue, purple, rose, or white flowers

<u>Carlisle, Jeremy</u>
acrid – bitter
lofty – high, elevated
tintypes – a type of photograph made on an iron plate

<u>Carman, Eugene</u>
gingham – a type of dyed fabric
sodden – soggy
transom – a type of window

<u>Church, John M.</u>
indemnity – compensation, reimbursement
thereat – there

<u>Churchill, Alfonso</u>
ebon – ebony, dark black in color
jeered – taunted, mocked
lunar – having to do with the moon
quadrillions – one thousand times one trillion

<u>Clapp, Homer</u>
bade – bid, offered
revival – a religious meeting that consists of passionate preaching

<u>Compton, Seth</u>
vestige – evidence

<u>Culbertson, E.C.</u>
oblivion – being forgotten

D
<u>Davidson, Robert</u>
nephritis – a condition in which the kidneys become inflamed

Dement, Silas
portico – a porch or walkway

Dobyns, Batterton
boutonniére – a flower worn through a shirt's buttonhole or on the pocket of a
  jacket
ruddy – rosy colored

Drummer, Hare
vales – a valley

Dunlap, Enoch
rabble – a person of the lowest social class

E
Ehrenhardt, Imanuel
rapturous – having extreme joy

F
Fallas, State's Attorney
inexorable – unstoppable, relentless
scourge-wielder – one who handles a whip
smiter – inflictor, the person who inflicts punishment on others

Ferguson, Wallace
yore – days gone by

Fluke, Willard
congregation – the church community
Foote, Searcy
gourmand – a glutton

Ford, Webster
burgeoning – blossoming
coronal – wreaths worn on the head
derided – ridiculed
lambent – glowing, bright
laurel – a type of evergreen tree
sere – dry

Fraser, Benjamin
gilt – golden in color

G
Garber, James
kindred – family members
reproach – to criticize, reprimand

Gardner, Samuel
aeolian – [*eolian*] carried by the breeze
umbrageous – shady

Garrick, Amelia
vanquished – defeated

Godbey, Jacob
ascetic – people who lead their lives with self-discipline and self-denial in an attempt to reach spiritual enlightenment
insolent – angry
strumpet – a promiscuous woman
Goldman, Le Roy
revivalist – a person who leads religious revivals (ceremonies or acts used to restore or revive religious faith)

Goode, William
zeal – enthusiasm

Goodhue, Harry Carey
prohibition – the act of refusing (usually referring to the manufacturing and selling of alcohol)
smote – attacked

Goodpasture, Jacob
battlements – protective barriers, fortifications
brood – a group, family
wooing – begging, pleading

Gray, George
furled – rolled in

Green, Ami
jest – a joke

Greene, Hamilton
vivacity – liveliness

Griffy the Cooper
cooper – a craftsman who repairs and constructs wooden barrels and tubs
dispel – to drive away, chase away
staves – wooden strips used to form the sides of tubs or barrels

Gustine, Dorcas
berate – to criticize, scold
remonstrance – complaints, protests
transgressed – committed sins; trespassed

H
Hainsfeather, Barney
excursion – roundtrip, journey

Hamblin, Carl
brandishing – waving
imploringly – pleadingly

Hately, Constance
benefactions – kind deeds
censure – to criticize

Hatfield, Aaron
hewers – one who cuts with an ax

Hawley, Jeduthan
sepulchral – relating to a burial vault or funeral ceremony

Henry, Chase
redounded – contributed, added

Herndon, William H.
dithyramb – a type of poem with an irregular beat
sovereign – supreme; independent

Heston, Roger
gored – pierced, stabbed

Higbie, Archibald
aspire – to strive
nativity – birth

Houghton, Jonathan
thrush – a type of bird

Howard, Jefferson
audacity – boldness
charnel – suitable for housing the dead
dankness – dampness
prestige – respect
reaping – to obtain, gather
valiant – brave

Hueffer, Cassius
epitaph – the inscription on a tombstone

Humphrey, Lydia
democratized – to make a democracy (a government ruled by the people through
     elected representatives)
disdaining – hating
spire – the steeple of a church

Hurley, Scholfield
keels – ships

Hutchins, Lambert
metropolis – a major city
obelisk – a type of stone that has a pointed top
spires – steeple-like structures

I
—

J

James, Godwin
alchemy – the study of chemistry
shorn – cut; removal
smitten – affected by something

Joe, Plymouth Rock
esotericism – mysteries
midges – types of birds
raucous – harsh, rough sounding

Jones, Fiddler
bassoons – a type of wind instrument, similar to a clarinet
beeves – plural of *beef*
drouth – [*drought*] a long period with little or no rainfall

Jones, "Indignation"
indignation – furious, annoyed

Jones, Minerva
jeered – taunted, teased

Jones, William
rue – a type of tropical plant (in the form of a shrub or small tree)

Judge, The Circuit
intangible – pretend, imaginable

K

Karr, Elmer
penitent – shameful, sorrowful

Kessler, Bert
brier – a type of thorny plant
plummet – tumble, plunge

Kessler, Mrs.
napery – a type of table cloth

Killion, Captain Orlando
blasphemer – a person who speaks profanely (in regard to religion)
captaincy – having the rank of captain
centaur – a mythological creature that is half man, half horse
dauntless – brave
fledglings – a beginner, novice
precipice – a steep cliff
reverently – respectfully, in a worshiping fashion

Kincaid, Russell
girded – surrounded

Knapp, Nancy
granary – a building for storing grain
murrain – a highly contagious disease of cattle

Konovaloff, Ippolit
architectonics – the science of architecture
eke – to make

L
—

M
M'Cumber, Daniel
dilettante – a person whose interest is only superficial
solace – comfort

McDowell, Rutherford
ambrotypes – the process of photographing during the mid 1800s
fathom – to imagine
pathos – a feeling (usually sorrow, sympathy, or pity)

McGee, Fletcher
pensive – thoughtful

McGee, Ollie
avenged – punished
haggard – worn, skinny

M'Grew, Jennie
gleaned – gathered

McGuire, Jack
lynched – executed without permission from the courts

McNeely, Mary
repose – a rest

McNeely, Paul
winsome – charming

McNeely, Washington
debauch – corruption
dowered – money or property a bride gives to her husband when they marry
invalided – incapacitated by illness
recluse – a hermit, one who withdraws from social activity

Marsh, Zilpha
crooned – hummed, sang softly

eddy – a current (air or water) moving in a spiral motion

flue – the pipe that carries smoke from the fireplace to the chimney

planchette – a board that, when touched lightly with fingertips, is said to convey supernatural messages (similar to a Ouija board)

Marshall, Herbert
wantonness – cruelty, wickedness

Matheny, Faith
ether – a type of flammable liquid once used as an anesthetic

lambent – bright

Metcalf, Willie
livery – most likely referring to the horse stable (a *livery* was a person who was hired to care for the horses and the stables)

Meyers, Doctor
congenial – friendly, pleasant

improvident – careless, reckless

indicted – accused, charged

Meyers, Mrs.
admonition – a warning; advice

Micure, Hamlet
diphtheria – a bacterial disease, which has flu-like symptoms but can lead to more serious complications, such as swelling of the heart, paralysis, or death

mullioned – framed in such a way (with stone or wood) to divide a window or other opening

verandah – a porch, balcony

Miller, Julia
estranged – alienated

verily – truthfully

Miner, Georgine Sand
cunning – skillful deception

embittering – evoking bitter or sour feelings

flaneur – an idler; one who wanders aimlessly

harlot – a promiscuous woman

parasite – one who lives off others

radical – a person who wants extreme governmental or societal change

squaw-man – a derogatory term for a man (who is *not* of Native American decent) who has a Native American wife and lives with her people

Moir, Alfred
errant – wandering

garish – flashy, gaudy

N

Nutter, Isa

leucæmia – [*leukemia*] a cancerous disease of the bone marrow

satyriasis – [*satyriasis*] a condition in which the patient (typically male) had an uncontrollable sexual desire

O

Osborne, Mabel

chasteness – purity

Otis, John Hancock

veritable – genuine

P

Pantier, Benjamin

aspiration – ambition, desire

comrade – a friend, companion

snared – trapped

solace – a comfort

Pantier, Mrs. Benjamin

loathe – to hate

Pantier, Reuben

amorous – passionate, loving, romantic

cocotte – a promiscuous woman, prostitute

milliner – a person who designs and creates hats

peril – danger, threat

Peet, Rev. Abner

grog – a type of liquor

Penniwit, the Artist

patronage – support

Petit, the Poet

constancy – faithfulness

iambics – iambic pentameter; a verse or line of poetry that has ten syllables and every second beat is accented

rondeaus – similar to a rondel; a poem with 10 or 13 lines with only two rhyming lines—the opening lines are repeated twice

rondels – a poem of 13 or 14 lines with only two rhyming lines throughout; the first line reappears at the end of the poem

triolets – poems or verses that consist of very specific elements; a triolet has a rhyme scheme of *abaaabab*, the fourth and seventh line are the same as the first line, and the eighth line is the same as the second line.

valor – bravery

villanelles – a poem with 19 lines, five tercets (a group of three lines that usually rhyme), some rhymes in the tercets are alternated and end with a couplet

Phipps, Henry
dupe – a fool

Pollard, Edmund
anthers – the part of the flower that contains the pollen
sidle – to ease in gradually or carefully

Potter, Cooney
toiling – pushing oneself to perform hard labor

Purkapile, Roscoe
dispensation – an assignment
lark – a carefree adventure

Putt, Hod
toil – conflict, strife

R
Reece, Mrs. George
unscrupulous – unethical, corrupt
vain – arrogant, conceded

Rhodes, Ralph
acrid – unpleasant smelling
demireps – a person with a questionable reputation

Rhodes, Thomas
erratic – inconsistent

Richter, Gustav
etherealized – made delicate or light; heavenly
immanent – existing in the mind

Ross, Thomas, Jr.
shrike – a type of bird with a hooked beak, which it uses to impale its prey

Russian Sonia
betimes – ahead
sundry – various

Rutledge, Anne
beneficent – kind, goodhearted

S
Sayre, Johnnie
remorseless – unforgiving, merciless
smote – inflicted, damaged
solace – comfort
truant – to play hooky; to be absent from

Sersmith the Dentist
chattel – an object of personal property; a slave
martyred – sacrificed
odes – a type of poem or song
reformations – improvements

Sewall, Harlan
ministrations – assistance
wormwood – a type of plant used in flavoring wine

Shelley, Percy Bysshe
snipe – a type of bird with a long beak

Shope, Tennessee Claflin
efficacy – effectiveness
rheumatism – pain in the joints, similar to arthritis
sovereignty – superiority

Sibley, Amos
fortitude – strength
loathed – hated
termagant – an argumentative, nagging woman; a shrew
wanton – an immoral person

Siever, Conrad
chemic – chemical

Sissman, Dillard
zenith – the highest point

Slack, Margaret Fuller
lock-jaw – a condition in which the jaw becomes locked due to a muscle spasm
untoward – not favorable

Smith, Louise
clematis – a type of climbing plant with various colored blossoms
seminary – a private school for girls
tendrils – vines

Soldiers, Many
sundered – separated

Somers, Judge
erudite – scholarly, learned

Sparks, Emily
aflame – interested
aright – correctly
dross – the waste or impure material

Standard, W. Lloyd Garrison
orator – speaker
whelp – a child

Stewart, Lillian
dowry – the monetary goods brought by a bride to her husband when they are wed
grist-mill – a grain mill
vexed – upset

T
Taylor, Deacon
cirrhosis – a disease that infects the liver, usually caused by excessive alcohol consumption, infection, or malnutrition

Theodore the Poet
turbid – muddy
wanes – approaches an end

Thornton, English
figurants – female ballet dancers
legislatures – officials elected to make laws

Throckmorton, Alexander
conflagration – a large and destructive fire
divination – telling the future, predicting
prophecy – a prediction

Todd, Eugenia
thwarted – hindered

Tompkins, Josiah
hindrance – a bother, annoyance
solace – comfort

Trainor, the Druggist
miser – a collector

Trevelyan Thomas
thurible – a container used to burn incense during religious ceremonies

Trimble, George
morality – goodness, decency

Tubbs, Hildrup
gonfalon – a banner or flag that represents royalty
lusts – cravings, desires
misanthropical – to become a person who hates mankind
putrescent – rotten, decomposing, foul
saprophyte – something that survives off of dead or decaying matter

Turner, Francis
acadia – a type of tree with white flowers
catalpa – a type of tree with white, yellow, or purple flowers

Tutt, Oaks
necropolis – [Greek] "city of the dead"; a large, elaborate cemetery

U
Unknown, The
guttural – from the gut, deep
wanton – reckless, careless

W
Wasson, John
scourges – suffering

Webster, Charles
russet – reddish-brown in color
spire – the top (usually referring to a pointed top, like a steeple, or in this case, the pine tree)
tremolo – the effect produced by the repetition of a single tone
whip-poor-wills – a type of nocturnal bird

Weirauch, Adam
anarchists – radicals
denounced – accused

Weldy, "Butch"
heave – to swell

Whedon, Editor
clandestine – secretive
demoniac – having to do with the devil; evil
paranoiac – paranoid
sneak-thief – a thief who can steal without having to force his entry by breaking windows or doors or using violence

Whitney, Harmon
paramour – a lover, especially one involved in adultery
yokels – unsophisticated people

Wiley, Rev. Lemuel
converts – people who choose to change religions later in life
revivals – religious meetings that consist of passionate preaching

Williams, Dora
insidious – cunning, sinister
magnate – an influential person

Williams, Mrs.
milliner – a person who creates, designs, and repairs hats

Wilmans, Harry
assailed – attacked
degradation – mortification, humiliation

Witt, Zenas
stammered – stuttered

Y
—

Z
—

The Spooniad
clique – a crowd
coadjutor – an assistant
concubine – a woman living with a man without being married to him
daub – a picture
duffer – an incompetent person
eminence – a nobleman, leader
engendered – existing
fain – happily; ready
fastidious – meticulous
guile – deceit
hecatombs – sacrifices
inspiriting – encouraging
jocund – lighthearted
lackeys – servants; followers
lamentations – cries of sorrow and grief, mourning
laureate – an honored poet
libertines – people who act freely
loathed – detested
pallor – extremely pale
paunch – the belly
proscenium – an area in a theater between the curtain and the orchestra
pyres – large heaps of flammable elements used for burning a corpse at a funeral
ribaldry – profanity
salve – to soothe, heal, ease
smite – to strike
strife – a quarrel
supine – inactive
thronged – crowded
trice – an instant
trod – walked
vacillation – hesitation
wanton – rebellious
zealous – enthusiastic, excited

Epilogue
allegorical – symbolic
atheism – the belief in no god or religion
benedictory – a blessing, prayer
brayed – crushed
cataclysm – a momentous change
creeds – systems of belief (usually referring to Christianity)
cyclorama – a picture that expands around the entire room
deckers – tiers, levels
defiles – pollutes
distrait – preoccupied
dumb – mute
enmesh – to entangle
hallows – devotes
hoary – gray or white in color
jest – a witty or smart remark
laborious – extremely difficult
lore – tradition, facts, beliefs
martyrdom – the act of being sacrificed
mucin – an element found in mucous membranes
nasturtium – a type of plant that produces an odorous juice
nomenclature – the system of determining scientific names
paradox – something containing contradictory elements
pestle – a bar, club (stick)
phantasmagoria – a hallucination, dream
prognosticate – to predict
rout – to defeat
scourge – a punishment
scrofula – a type of tuberculosis that affects the lymph nodes in the neck; the disease is usually spread through infected cattle
solace – comfort
thwart – to hinder
upas – a type of tree used in making poison

Insightful and Reader-Friendly, Yet Affordable

Prestwick House Literary Touchstone Editions–
The Editions By Which All Others May Be Judged

Every Prestwick House Literary Touchstone Edition™ is enhanced with Reading Pointers for Sharper Insight to improve comprehension and provide insights that will help students recognize key themes, symbols, and plot complexities. In addition, each title includes a Glossary of the more difficult words and concepts.

For the Shakespeare titles, along with the Reading Pointers and Glossary, we include margin notes and eleven strategies to understanding the language of Shakespeare.

New titles are constantly being added; call or visit our website for current listing.

Special Introductory Educator's Discount – At Least 50% Off

		Retail Price	Intro. Discount
200102	Red Badge of Courage, The	$3.99	$1.99
200163	Romeo and Juliet	$3.99	$1.99
200074	Heart of Darkness	$3.99	$1.99
200079	Narrative of the Life of Frederick Douglass	$3.99	$1.99
200125	Macbeth	$3.99	$1.99
200053	Adventures of Huckleberry Finn, The	$4.99	$2.49
200081	Midsummer Night's Dream, A	$3.99	$1.99
200179	Christmas Carol, A	$3.99	$1.99
200150	Call of the Wild, The	$3.99	$1.99
200190	Dr. Jekyll and Mr. Hyde	$3.99	$1.99
200141	Awakening, The	$3.99	$1.99
200147	Importance of Being Earnest, The	$3.99	$1.99
200166	Ethan Frome	$3.99	$1.99
200146	Julius Caesar	$3.99	$1.99
200095	Othello	$3.99	$1.99
200091	Hamlet	$3.99	$1.99
200231	Taming of the Shrew, The	$3.99	$1.99
200133	Metamorphosis, The	$3.99	$1.99

PRESTWICK HOUSE, INC.
"Everything for the English Classroom!"

Prestwick House, Inc. • P.O. Box 658, Clayton, DE 19938
Phone (800) 932-4593 • Fax (888) 718-9333 • www.prestwickhouse.com